SPOKANE

Pictorial Research by David Reynolds

American Historical Press
Sun Valley, California

SPOKANE

A VIEW OF THE FALLS

An Illustrated History
By William Stimson

Page two: *Spokane Falls in 1884 as recreated by artist William Donohue in 1944. Courtesy, Northwest Room, Spokane Public Library*

Page three: *A small parade drew a crowd on Riverside in this circa 1911 photo. The wagons are crossing the intersection of Riverside and Washington. Courtesy, Northwest Room, Spokane Public Library*

© American Historical Press
All Rights Reserved
Published 1999
Printed in the United States of America

Library of Congress Catalogue Card Number: 99-75346

ISBN: 1-892724-07-3

Bibliography: p. 186
Includes Index

CONTENTS

I

THE LAND AS FATE

Spokane's history begins deep in the earth, where the heat generated by the downward pressure of the earth's gravity creates immense caldrons of molten rock. When this magma—as the liquid rock is called—finds an avenue upward, it generally becomes trapped under the crust of the earth and creates a bulge—a mountain. The mountains north and east of Spokane were created by such forces hundreds of millions of years ago.

As the magma at the center of these newly created mountains cooled, it shriveled and cracked, leaving fissures like pipelines running to every part of the mountain. Super-heated water came boiling up from the core of the earth through these fissures, bringing with it dissolved gold, silver, lead, zinc and other minerals. Millions of years of such activity laced the mountains of this region with the riches that would one day re-direct Spokane history.

But it was magma that did not stop below the earth's surface that created most of what we see. Some 15 million years ago, in an event unique to geological history, cracks in the earth's surface ranging in size from a few feet to a few yards began opening up in what is now southeastern Washington and northeastern Oregon. Out of these fissures flowed oceans of syrupy molten rock in volumes sufficient to travel, in some cases, hundreds of miles. When it was all over, most of Eastern Washington and large sections of Oregon and Idaho were covered with the reddish-brown basalt a mile thick on the average. All the land in the vicinity of Spokane stood at the level of

Five Mile Prairie and the South Hill. Then the river began to chisel itself a new channel, creating after 12 million years of work, the Spokane Valley.

Sometimes the river found a layer of basalt more resistant than usual. It passed over this rock and continued its drilling beyond, leaving a shelf for the water to spill over. This is how the Spokane falls was created. Meanwhile the prevailing southwest winds were dusting the basalt with a rich silt, laying down, bit by bit, the dune-like hills of the Palouse. Going back millions of years, but as recently as 1980, the volcanos to the west periodically exploded and contributed wind-borne minerals which make the Palouse soil extraordinary.

Long after the lava flows, just 10,000 to 15,000 years ago, the region was altered by another, more sudden, cataclysm. A cooling in the earth's climate created many immense glaciers in this area. One of these huge accumulations of ice blocked a canyon and stopped the flow of Montana's Clark Fork River into the Pend Oreille Lake. The river water backed up for dozens of years and filled three long canyons covering much of western Montana.

Suddenly the glacier holding back all this water gave way. The result was the greatest flood ever to occur on earth. An estimated 500 cubic miles of water surged down the Rathdrum valley, across the area of Spokane and down the center of Washington State.

As a strong stream from a garden hose plucks out and carries pebbles with it, so this deluge carried rocks and boulders it

Basalt chutes line the old Sunset Highway, west of Spokane. An ocean of lava once covered the Inland Empire. When it cooled it cracked vertically, leaving the pillar-like designs where humans or nature cut through it. (EWSHS)

had collected on its route. Some of the material built up dams across small valleys east of Spokane, causing the water of their streams to accumulate. This created a whole series of lakes, including Coeur d'Alene, Hayden, Liberty, and Newman. Other rocks brought by the flood settled in the Rathdrum and Spokane valley floors. Covered over eventually by a layer of soil, these rocks formed the filter-like underground stream or "aquifer" from which the city of Spokane would get its water.

It happened that the area of present Spokane was already covered by an immense glacial lake when this deluge

struck, so its features were cushioned from the violence. The higher land southwest of the city had no such protection, and the floodwaters splashed upon it like a bucket of water upon a dusty sidewalk. The soil was scrubbed away, leaving behind Eastern Washington's sculpturesque but nearly barren "scablands." The turbulence of the water was such that it even plucked out basalt in places, creating the basins of the lakes south and west of Spokane.

We do not know if human beings were present to witness—or perhaps be swept away by—this colossal flood. But man was at least nearby. It was about the

8

time of the last of the floods, about 10,000 years ago, that the young man found in the Marmes burial site (named for the modern-day owner of the land) was buried in a canyon about fifty miles west of Pullman. It could not have been long, given the nomadic ways of such tribes, before similar groups lived in the Spokane area.

Virtually nothing is known about the progress of the Indians from the time of their Ice Age arrival to the time when whites discovered them inhabiting this area. Through their own Pasteurs and Edisons, however, they had triumphed over their environment. Instead of shiver-ing against the cold under a pile of brush, as his ancestors had, the modern Indian had learned to live in a snug cone-shaped shelter, large enough to allow comfort, small enough to be kept warm by a small fire. Instead of foraging daily for scraps of food to keep him alive, he had become so efficient at gathering and preserving foods that he could go through a harsh winter without stirring from his tent if he didn't care to. His style of life was pleasant and secure. On the whole, the common-rank Spokane Indian of, say, 1500 A.D. was in all probability safer, healthier, and better fed than his European counterpart.

These pictographs were painted by the Spokane Indians on a cave wall near the Little Spokane River (shown here as they appeared in 1920). Today the earth-colored paintings are nearly obliterated by vandalism. Although many such drawings have been found throughout the Northwest, the meaning of the designs is not known. (EWSHS)

In the 1870s more than 3,000 Spokanes lived in small villages scattered across the area. The name "Spokanee" means "Children of the Sun," and refers to the three Spokane tribes. The upper tribe was located near Lake Coeur d'Alene, the middle around what is now Spokane, and the lower tribe camped at the mouth of the Spokane River. (EWSHS)

What the Indians had discovered over the thousands of years, while Europeans experimented with agriculture, was that the land, if one knew how to use it, would easily support a small population. Locating, harvesting, and preserving fruits, seeds, herbs, trees, bark, leaves, and mushrooms constituted a virtual botanical science—and one that had to be mastered by each Indian family. Modern botanists have discovered at least 200 natural growing products used by the Indians of this area. Soapberries, for example, are bitter; but placed in a bowl with a few wild strawberries for sweetening and whipped, they became a tasty pink froth called "Indian ice cream" that was served to guests. A tea made from the same bush was used as a medicine for an upset stomach. The leaves, when boiled, produced a popular shampoo.

Gathering these products through the year was pleasant and varied employment. In early spring when the snow was gone an Indian village of several hundred people would dismantle its winter camp (which was usually near a river) and divide up into small family groups. Each would go into its own traditional fields to begin the harvest of spring plants.

The whole tribe, and often members from other tribes, would gather again in June by the river to fish for salmon. Spawning salmon once swam all the way to the Spokane falls, and catching them there with spears and nets, then cleaning and drying them for storage, was a major industry that employed hundreds, all taking orders from a "salmon chief."

When the salmon season was over the Indians would strike their tents and move to the damp meadows to gather

The annual return of the salmon to the Spokane falls inspired an Indian celebration. Each summer well-organized groups gathered at prime locations up and down the riverbanks to spear spawners. Construction of mammoth hydroelectric dams on the Spokane and Columbia rivers ended the salmon runs in the 1930s. (EWSHS)

camas, a root that was baked and eaten as bread. When autumn came the Indians once again scattered in smaller groups to go to the hills to pick berries. Families went to the same gullies and clearings year after year, and so took care of them as they would their own farms. They never over-harvested and they employed many techniques for keeping the bushes productive—they knew, for example, that breaking a huckleberry stem at just the right place would make two berries grow instead of one the next season.

In the fall and winter the men hunted deer, bear, and other game. The hunt of buffalo, an animal which existed in large numbers only east of the Rocky Moun-

tains, provided the Spokanes and Coeur d'Alenes with their annual adventure into Blackfeet country, where all intruders were attacked as a matter of policy. Except for these forays, the Spokanes, Coeur d'Alenes and other small tribes of this immediate area were different from most Indian tribes—and most human civilizations—in that they lived virtually without war. Their dealings with other tribes were in the form of trade. The Spokanes and Coeur d'Alenes served as middlemen, trading dried salmon for buffalo hides with the Blackfeet, then trading the hides for shells, wood carvings and other products of the coastal Indians.

Early in the nineteenth century Euro-

Right: *Father Joseph Joset, S.J., shown here in 1870, was priest to the Coeur d'Alene Indians, and with fellow Jesuits, founder of the Mission of the Sacred Heart. Joset was instrumental in arranging a temporary cease-fire between the tribes and Colonel Edward Steptoe's dragoons during the latter's retreat. Later, during Colonel George Wright's punitive action, Joset was able to secure more lenient conditions for the Coeur d'Alenes. (EWSHS)*

Right: *Listed in the National Register of Historic Places, Cataldo Mission is the oldest known standing building in the state of Idaho. Shown here in the 1920s, the mission has been reconstructed several times since 1928. (EWSHS)*

pean men took to decorating themselves with hats made of beaver furs. Meeting the demand for the pelts of these little animals was the enterprise that brought white civilization among the Northwest Indians. In 1810 the North West Company, a Canadian firm, established the first of several trading posts that would operate where the Spokane River meets the Little Spokane River.

The first missionaries to the area, the Reverends Elkanah Walker and Cushing Eells, arrived with their wives in 1838 and built a small mission on the Walla Walla-Colville Road, near what is now Ford, Washington. The accommodating Indians converted in large numbers and then went on living more or less as they always had. "We have been here almost nine years," Mrs. Eells admitted to her diary, "and have not been permitted to hear the cries of one penitent, or the songs of one redeemed soul." Later missionaries, notably the trusted Reverend

Henry T. Cowley and the tireless Jesuits Pierre De Smet, Joseph Joset and Joseph Cataldo, would do better by taking the time to learn the Indians' way of life and meeting them half way.

Over a period of four decades, the Indians gradually became accustomed to the whites. From the traders they were happy to acquire guns, factory-made knives, traps, and tobacco. From the missionaries they took a little Christianity without, as Mrs. Eells lamented, altering their lives unduly. Among the diaries, letters, and memoirs of the time, it's hard to find a white with much bad to say of the Spokanes and Coeur d'Alenes. Where they are recorded on the subject, the Indians professed to find the whites friendly and reliable.

But inevitably there would come a crisis. The Willamette Valley not so far to the south was the termination point of the Oregon Trail. By the 1850s the Willamette and adjacent valleys were already beginning to fill up with homesteaders and miners. The white culture, instead of being an aspect of life in the region, was swiftly becoming life itself. The Indians of the Northwest were in good communication, and all the tribes to the north heard what was happening to the Indians of the Willamette Valley as whites came. One entire tribe, the Klikitats, had been removed by the U.S. Army to Yakima country. No tribe could remain impassive in the face of such stories. Some renegades in what is now central Oregon had already commenced guerrilla warfare by indiscriminately attacking wagon trains, miners, and other white targets.

In 1853, Isaac I. Stevens was given the dual title of governor of Washington Territory (the territory's first) and Superintendent of Indian Affairs for the new territory. His most important assignment was to make the area safe for settlement by winning treaties with the Indians.

Stevens had the kind of brilliance and

Left: *Located twenty-five miles northeast of Spokane at Ford, Tshimakain (Chemakane) was the first Protestant mission in northeastern Washington. This lithograph was drawn by J.M. Stanley in 1853, about four years after the Reverends Elkanah Walker and Cushing Eells had closed the mission. Stanley accompanied Isaac Stevens on his expedition across the territory and his drawings provided Congress with their first pictures of the Pacific Northwest. (EWSHS)*

Right: *Governor Isaac Stevens was appointed first territorial governor of Washington in 1853. Stevens' major tasks were to organize a civil government in the territory and treat with the Indian tribes. He was elected a delegate to Congress from the territory in 1857 and was killed in the Civil War a few years later. (EWSHS)*

Far right: *Hudson's Bay Company sent Spokane Garry to Fort Garry (now Winnipeg, Manitoba) in 1825. He learned to read, write, and speak English, and was converted to Christianity. Five years later he returned as the first Protestant missionary to the Spokane Indians. Garry also built the first school in Spokane and became its first teacher. (EWSHS)*

ambition that could put a person out of sync with the rest of the human race. He had graduated first in his West Point class and then had plunged into a series of army assignments with such vigor and imagination that it alternately thrilled and outraged superiors. Within a year of his appointment he had concluded treaties with most of the coastal tribes. A few months later, on May 29, 1855, he had representatives of many interior tribes assembled at a council at Walla Walla. The Spokanes and Coeur d'Alenes were not involved in these negotiations but, knowing they would be next to deal with Stevens, they sent Chief Spokane Garry to observe.

Stevens, always impatient and decisive, had already drawn on a map the reservations that were to be offered. Wagons, blankets and other inducements were to be thrown into the deal. But he insisted the treaties be signed there and then. The Indians signed. But many of them were dissatisfied with the size and locations of their assigned reservations. Instead of instruments of peace, Stevens'

treaties became a focus of resentment among most Indians. If Stevens had not already realized this, it was made clear to him by the Spokanes when he visited them in December of 1855. "I had there," Stevens recalled later in his meticulous record of the meetings, "one of the most stormy councils for three days that had ever occurred in my whole Indian experience."

One chief after another rose to say that he did not want war, but Stevens' own behavior at the Walla Walla council was making it difficult to argue for peace. Spokane Garry chided Stevens for his high-handed attitude toward Indians:

When you look at the red men, you think you have more heart, more sense, than these poor Indians. I think the difference between us and you Americans is in the clothing: the blood and body are the same. Do you think, because your mother was white and their's dark, that you are higher or better? We are dark, yet if we cut ourselves, the blood will be red, and with the whites it is the same, though their skin is white. I do not think we are poor because we belong to another nation. If you take those Indians for men, treat them so now.

Chiefs of both the Spokane and Coeur d'Alene tribes made two things clear to Stevens. The first was that they had no intention of joining the other tribes in the area which were even then making war against the whites. The second was that, until there was a treaty, whites must respect Indian borders.

The army, which in these years frequently had more sympathy for the Indian side than that of the whites, knew

to join the war. Many important chiefs, including Garry of the Spokanes and Victor of the Coeur d'Alenes, argued for peace. But the call of Kamiakin for Indians to stand together now or die was persuasive to many others. Kamiakin was arguing that eventually white soldiers would come and force the Spokanes and Coeur d'Alenes into exile.

Then, on May 6, 1858, Colonel Steptoe decided to take four companies of cavalry from Walla Walla to Colville to assess the fears of some white settlers who felt they were in danger from Indians. Knowing of the friendly relations between the whites and Indians of this region, Steptoe was

As whites expanded the township of Spokane Falls, the main Spokane tribe moved further west to where Latah (Hangman) Creek empties into the river. Teepees could still be seen in that area, known as Indian Canyon, up to the 1920s. These Spokanes were camped in Peaceful Valley, west of the Spokane River falls, circa 1880. (EWSHS)

that Stevens' treaties were causing the problem. Colonel Edward Steptoe, commander of the fort at Walla Walla, told his superiors that in his opinion enforcing the treaties, "will be followed by immediate hostilities with most of the tribes in this part of the country; for which reason it does appear to me greatly desirable that a new commission be appointed, and a new treaty made, thoroughly digested and accepted by both sides."

Meanwhile, Kamiakin, a chief of the Yakimas and leader of the Indian resistance, came among the Spokanes and Coeur d'Alenes to try to persuade them

skeptical of the reports of imminent uprisings. But about halfway on through his journey, in the rolling hills of the grass-covered Palouse hills (north of the present Colfax), he was surprised to look up and find the crests of the hills lined with Indians in war regalia. Steptoe met with the chiefs and assured them he meant them no harm. They apparently accepted his word, but some excited braves had begun to taunt the soldiers. Some shots were fired. In defending themselves the soldiers soon killed a chief of the Coeur d'Alenes and several other Indians, causing the Indian mood to turn from cockiness to hot anger. After a two-day running battle (May 16 and 17) Steptoe led his men to the refuge of a hill. As night fell, the whole command of 156—two company officers had already fallen—was surrounded by approximately 1,000 Indians. Then it was discovered that so little ammunition had been packed that each of Steptoe's soldiers had only about four rounds left. It looked as if the command would be easily overwhelmed come morning. But in the dark of the night Steptoe and his men managed the now famous escape through the lines of the sleeping Indians.

What an irony that Steptoe, who, like many army officers at the time, sympathized with the Indian cause, and the Spokanes and Coeur d'Alenes, the most peaceable tribes in the territory, should have ended up destroying each other in this accidental and meaningless little battle. Steptoe, whose health had been fragile already, never recovered from the rigorous march of escape and soon retired from the army, a virtual invalid. The Spokanes and Coeur d'Alenes would always mark this two days of battle as the opening of an era of endless heartbreak.

The Jesuits who lived among the Coeur d'Alenes tried to mediate before there was more violence. But it was too late for amicable solutions. Three months later, Colonel George Wright rode out the gate of Fort Walla Walla at the head of a force of 570 regulars and 30 Nez Perce scouts, heading north to get revenge.

On August 31, 1858, Wright's troops made their camp at Basset Spring, halfway between the present towns of Medical Lake and Cheney. The following morning the soldiers awoke to find a group of Indians at the top of a hill two miles to the north. Wright eagerly deployed his troops in two sections, like a two-handed grab at the hill, but the Indians fled down the far side. When Wright and his officers reached the crest of the hill they saw hundreds of Indians below. On order, the well-drilled infantry pressed down upon the Indian formation until it shattered into fleeing individuals. At that moment, the dragoons, who had been leading their horses at a walk behind the infantry, mounted and galloped after the Indians. Lieutenant Lawrence Kip, who was watching with Wright from the top of the hill, said in his diary: "We saw the flash of their sabers as they cut them down. Lt. Davidson shot one warrior from his saddle as they charged up, and Lt. Gregg clove the skull of another. Yells and shrieks and uplifted hands were of no avail as they rode over them."

A few days later the Spokanes again threw themselves in front of Wright's advance, using the distraction of grass fires (on land now occupied by Fairchild Air Force Base) to get closer to the soldiers. But Wright quickly analyzed the danger and ordered his troops to attack through the flames. This "Battle of Spokane Plains," like the previous "Battle of Four Lakes," hardly deserved the distinction of a name. In the whole campaign Wright's only battle casualty was one wounded man. The Indians' campfire enthusiasm and dash-in-and-shoot tactics were no match for those who made a profession and science of war.

While he was camped on a bluff overlooking the Spokane River (a site which forty years later would be occupied by Fort George Wright), Wright received word that Chief Spokane Garry wanted to talk. The two met on the river bank, near where the Mission Street Bridge is now. Wright told Garry that if the Indians wanted peace, "You must come with your arms, with your women and children, and everything you have, and lay them at my feet; you must put your faith in me and trust to my mercy." Otherwise, Wright said, he would "exterminate" the tribe. This was the very word he used.

Garry took Wright's terms back to the Spokanes while Wright turned east, toward the territory of the Coeur d'Alene Indians. The soldiers happened to capture a herd of 800 Indian horses near what is now the Idaho border. Horses were both the wealth and the war machines of the Indians. Unable to take them with him, Wright assigned two companies to slaughter them.

When Wright arrived in Coeur d'Alene country, that tribe immediately sued for peace. The colonel demanded total subjugation, took some prisoners, and returned eastward to accept the surrender of the Spokane tribe. The Spokanes surrendered on a site twenty miles to the southwest of the Spokane Falls, at a creek then called Latah.

Later that same day, September 24, 1855, Chief Owhi of the Yakimas rode in and gave himself up. Wright had him

put in irons and sent word to Owhi's son, a notorious killer of whites called Qualchan, that the father would be hanged if Qualchan did not also surrender immediately. Qualchan did come in the next morning, but apparently without having gotten Wright's message, because he acted surprised when he heard his father was already there. Why Qualchan came in, under a white flag, no one will ever know, because Wright had him dragged to a tree and hanged within minutes of his arrival. The following day, a large party of Palouse Indians came to the camp to surrender. Six of them were also hanged from nearby trees, and the stream that flows by the place has ever after been known as Hangman Creek in Wright's dubious honor.

The Spokanes, Coeur d'Alenes and other tribes of eastern Washington never again warred against whites. After they

Living in permanent dwellings, wearing white people's clothing, and cultivating crops, these Spokane Indian children at the Spokane reservation circa 1900 were forced to adopt a way of life that was previously unknown to their people. (EWSHS)

Spokane Indian Joe Robinson roasts meat the traditional way in 1900 in Indian Canyon. As the Indians were forced onto the reservations, much of their culture was diluted by white society. A handful of Spokanes, however, have taken an active part in preserving the language, arts, and traditions that were practiced by their people for hundreds of years. (EWSHS)

recovered from the loss of horses and food stores routinely destroyed by Wright's men, life for the Indians of the area returned almost to normal.

But twenty years later, all the things that had been foretold to the Indians, which had caused them to confront Steptoe's troops, suddenly came to pass. The railroads were approaching.

Father Alexander Diomedi, a Jesuit who had been working among the Coeur d'Alenes, called the men of that tribe together and warned them that whites would soon be so numerous that the fish, the game, and the prairies would disappear. If the Indians did not consent to go to a reservation and take up farming, Diomedi told them, "your children will starve; your wives and daughters will be unsafe; you yourselves will disappear."

The Indians were stunned. Finally, one

by the name of Alexander stood and said they had never required much to live and would not when the whites arrived. "You need bread, we have camas; you require good clothing, we are satisfied with deer skins and buffalo robes. We can live comfortably on what you think poor and wretched." Surely, Alexander thought, these few things would still be available to Indians after the whites came. They were finally persuaded otherwise by Diomedi, however, and the Coeur d'Alene tribe removed to its reservation in 1878.

The Spokane tribe reacted differently. It had to learn the hard way. The reservation for the Spokanes was established in 1881 (the same year the city of Spokane was incorporated and the first railroad reached it). But many Spokanes refused to sign a treaty and go there. Members of the tribe began picking out pieces of land around the city, prepared to live alongside the white man in the white man way. Some became good farmers and horse ranchers, but one by one all were pushed off their property. Timothy Brooks, one of the first white settlers near Deep Creek, southwest of Spokane, admitted that he himself had taken land occupied by Indians. Looking back in a 1925 interview Brooks said:

None of us in those days thought that an Indian had any rights that a white man was bound to respect. The Indians didn't know anything about the homestead laws and regulations and no one was anxious to put them wise. There were always little technicalities which one could raise against an Indian's claim with a good prospect of winning out against the Indian in the land office, in case he showed fight and persisted in trying to hang on to the land he wanted. Looking back, it is quite possible that we weren't always quite fair to those Indians.

The tragedy of the Indians is suggested by the story of Garry. Despite his blunt talk to Stevens, Garry had always believed that whites and Indians would learn to live together peaceably. As a young boy he had been educated by whites (thus his Anglicized name) and taught Christianity to his fellow tribe members. He refused to go to war against Colonel Wright, even though his pacifism probably meant he would be killed by the Indians had they won.

In the 1870s he was forced off two different ranches by white settlers. He then settled with a small band of followers in Hangman Creek, but was harassed by rowdies from town. Garry's daughter Nellie approached Garvin Mouat, a homesteader whose land included what is now Indian Canyon Golf Course, and asked if the small band could pitch their tepees on his land. Mouat consented and

consequently got to know Garry in the last years of his life.

"Garry's wife was blind," Mouat recalled many years later, "and Garry used to take care of her. He would lift her on and off the horse, and for riding would tie her on the horse and lead the horse. He was very attentive to her. After Garry died I went into his tepee, where Garry's body was lying stretched out on an old bedtick and Garry's old wife, her face like parchment and her hands on his chest, was kneeling by his remains moaning." Garry is buried in Greenwood Cemetery, a short distance from where he spent the final years of his life.

By 1887 the Spokanes had seen the futility of trying to hold onto any of this land and consented to move down the river to the reservation. Twenty years later, Spokane historian William S. Lewis talked to seven Spokane chiefs and found them still troubled. Speaking through an interpreter, they said they had never received the farming equipment and cash payments they were promised to help them establish on the new land: "When we were driven from our lands we left our farms, our gardens, our hunting grounds, our fishing places, and the burial places of our fathers. When we were compelled to move onto the reservation it was like putting birds in a cage. All the time since we have been waiting for some white men to come and tell us what to do."

What to do was the problem. Everything the Indian thought, did or valued depended on his owning this land, and this land was lost to him.

But at the same time it was opened to others. Tens of thousands of people—in the eastern part of the United States, in Ireland, England, France, Germany and Italy, and even as far away as China— were hearing about the American West and beginning to dream of tying their own fates to it.

II

THE CITY BUILDERS

With the end of the Civil War in 1865 the move west had begun in earnest. The Willamette Valley, at the termination of the Oregon Trail, filled quickly and settlers pushed on to adjacent valleys, including the Yakima Valley. From Yakima the migration gravitated steadily north. At first settlers in the Palouse country stayed in the lowlands along streams, thinking the hills unsuitable for agriculture. But latecomers with little choice gave the hills a try and, after a season or two of struggle against the tough bunch grass sod, produced an excellent crop of wheat. It became axiomatic among farmers with some experience that wheat would grow anywhere there was bunch grass, and bunch grass was everywhere in this country.

A second kind of migration, one of miners, simultaneously began to push into the mountains of Spokane country. The first important gold strikes were made in the Okanogan to the north in 1874 and in the Coeur d'Alene to the east in 1878.

The first settlers and miners could replenish their supplies as they passed through old established military towns like Walla Walla and Colville. But when they found their homesteading and mining sites and went to work, they would need close-by places to buy their nails, flour, coffee and other provisions. This gave rise to a third category of Western pioneer: the city builder. Mining towns like Molson in the Okanogan and Burke in the Coeur d'Alene appeared overnight, and generally were abandoned just as quickly when the quality of the ore

slipped (which is why today's ghost towns were virtually all originally mining towns). Farming towns—Rosalia, Colfax, Ritzville, Spangle, and many others still on the map—appeared wherever a couple of dozen farmers found they were more than a full day's round-trip ride to the next town.

The shopkeepers in these little settlements got their own supplies over a long, difficult route from Portland. The Northern Pacific Railroad, which was to connect them with all the big cities east and west, was temporarily stalled by financial difficulties. But when the railroad did arrive—and it was expected momentarily through the 1870s—it would be a boon to all these towns.

To one or two of them it would be more than that. It would be another kind of gold mine. It was clear that there would have to be a major distribution point in this inland area, a place where supplies coming in from east and west could be redistributed to all the communities north and south. With its rail links, this town would also likely become a regional manufacturing town and a center for superior law courts, major banks, hospitals, colleges, fine hotels and other urban amenities. Such a town was conspicuous by its absence between the Cascade and Rocky mountain ranges. Many of the new towns of the region fully expected to become metropolises when the railroad arrived.

To do so a town would have to fill two requirements. First, it would have to be within the corridor to be followed by the Northern Pacific line. Then, by growing

Spokane boomed as mining brought increasing white settlement. This is the primitive shaft house of Little Caribou Mine in the 1880s.(EWSHS)

faster than the others, it would have to establish itself as the logical resupply center for all the other towns.

Creating such a town was what James N. Glover and Jasper M. Matheny of Salem, Oregon, had in mind when they set out in the spring of 1873 to scout what was then known as "the wild interior." They rode north on horseback, looking over places where they might establish a new town and new lives. One evening in May the search brought them to the big falls in Spokane country, where a handful of people had set up a little sawmill and established squatter's rights. They were put up in one of the squatter's shacks, and the next morning Glover awoke early to go out and get a view of the falls he had heard thundering all night. He sat and watched the water for two hours, he said later, and when he went back for breakfast, drenched from the spray, he was convinced he had found his place. He and Matheny immediately bought out the squatters and returned to Portland for a bigger sawmill and supplies to open a

trading post.

But then, for months on end, not much happened at the little village generally called "the Falls." With no railroad to convey them, new settlers were few and scattered. In 1874, the Reverend Henry T. Cowley opened a school for Indians a short distance from the little store (on what is now Cowley Park). In 1875, the Reverend Samuel Havermale and his wife filed a claim for land that included the island that bears their name. A farmer drifted in here and there to join Moran, Liberty, Lefevre and the other sprinkling of early arrivals. But the new sawmill at the falls could still cut in a week all the lumber the settlers needed in a year. The railroad could save Glover's and Matheny's dream, but after three years there was still no sign of a building crew, and still no proof that the railroad would even come through the Falls.

By 1876 Matheny wanted out. Glover put up everything he had, plus promisory notes, to buy out Matheny and a third partner in Salem. Glover settled in to

continue the vigil by the falls alone. A passer-by of the time remembered this great enterprise, this metropolis of the future, as "a little store with some squaws sitting around the plank platform in front."

By the winter of 1877-1878 Glover still had enough confidence to engage a surveyor to lay out blocks and broad avenues in the fields of tall grass. Basing the whole town on the location of his store, Glover named the street to the north Front because it fronted on the river. (It would later be named Trent and then, just prior to the opening of Expo '74, Spokane Falls Boulevard.) The major north-south street he named for General Oliver O. Howard, the famous Indian fighter who that very winter was pursuing Chief Joseph's rebellious tribe. Glover explained that he had been standing on the platform on that side of the store when he first met General Howard. Glover envisioned the street one block back from the river as the town's center, so he called it Main. Riverside was originally named "South," but was later given

the name of its extension to the west, which followed the side of the river. Sprague was named for a general superintendent of the Northern Pacific, a gesture of flattery of the all-powerful railroad officials. Stevens commemorates the territory's first governor. Wall Street was originally called Mill because the sawmill was on the river there. Glover always regretted the change to the more pretentious name.

Post was named for Frederick Post, a German immigrant who moved his flour mill from Post Falls to Spokane Falls (as it was originally called) in 1877. How Post came to Spokane Falls tells something about Glover's determination and why his city survived. A flour mill would lure both sellers of wheat and buyers of flour to a city and was therefore much coveted by all the developing communities. Glover succeeded in persuading Post to move to Spokane Falls by offering the old man no less than a quarter of the whole town. On top of that, Glover donated the lumber for a new mill and helped with the construction.

The following spring, in April of 1878, two men from Portland were in the area scouting opportunities, just as Glover and Matheny had five years earlier. John

Left: *James N. Glover, shown here circa 1878, is known as the father of Spokane. Glover's enthusiasm and ingenuity helped to make Spokane the largest city in the Inland Northwest. In 1881 Glover built his second home on the site of the present Paulsen Medical building. Moved to the corner of First Avenue and Oak Street, Glover's house still stands as the oldest building in the city. (EWSHS)*

Below: *Glover's original 158 acres included most of the present downtown Spokane business district. He purchased the land for $2,000 in 1873, as recorded in this Official Registration of Land Title Patent issued to Glover on April 5, 1878. (EWSHS)*

Right: *Spokane Falls
had a total of seven
families when Port-
land, Oregon, attorney
J.J. Browne arrived in
1878. Like his partner
Anthony M. Cannon,
Browne envisioned a
potential population of
10,000. He founded the
First National Bank,
built the first street
railway, owned the
Spokane Chronicle,
and joined Cannon to
build the Auditorium
Theater. He donated
the land for Coeur
d'Alene Park in the
section of Spokane
that is his namesake,
Browne's Addition.*
(EWSHS)

J. Browne and his partner, Anthony
Cannon, decided to throw in with Glover.
For $3,200 (mostly on credit) they bought
half of Glover's remaining townsite.
Browne also filed a homestead claim for
land at the west edge of Glover's land—
"Browne's Addition"—and Cannon put
in a claim for land on the hill at the
south edge of town.

Browne, an attorney who had served a
term as superintendent of schools in
Portland, was levelheaded and ambitious.
Cannon was not so levelheaded but made
up for it by being twice as ambitious. He
was full of ideas, good ones and bad ones,
and history has been unkind to him
merely because he had an inclination toward the latter. Shortly after he arrived
he mistook wildflowers swaying in a night
breeze for feathers on Indians' heads and
got the whole village into an uproar with
warnings of an attack. It was probably
the last time he was ever overly cautious.
He opened the first bank in Spokane
Falls soon after arriving, but being considerably underfinanced, it was also the
first bank to go broke.

Cannon would have to be counted as
the main irritant as well as the main
booster of the little town—if it hadn't
been for the arrival of a feisty twenty-
eight-year-old editor by the name of
Francis Cook. Little wonder that the two
men were soon drawing swords. Cook
printed something (what it was we don't
know) that Cannon took exception to—
violent exception, as they say, because
Cannon and his son-in-law went to Cook's
offices with a loaded gun. Cook persuaded them to leave by belting them with a
press iron and kicking them down the
stairway.

An editor, even a bad tempered one,
was an impressive recruitment to the
city. Cook had come through on a general
inspection tour in 1879 and was charmed
by the place; Glover hooked him by donating both lots on the east side of Howard between Riverside and Sprague for
newspaper offices.

By now others were choosing to settle here without such inducements. Dr.
Joseph Gandy, a physician from Tacoma
seeking a drier climate, built an office on
Howard (with a second story for his family to live in) and gave Spokane a doc-
tor's services. Seattle's city attorney,
Colonel David P. Jenkins, defected to
Spokane in 1880. Jenkins, a dapper,
cane-carrying Civil War hero, was the

Left: *An ambitious pioneer and businessman, Anthony M. Cannon built the huge Auditorium Theater, founded the Spokane & Palouse Railroad, started the Bank of Spokane Falls, and presided as mayor of the city. (EWSHS)*

Far left: *This sawmill on the river near present-day Post Street Bridge, where James Glover turned out timber for the first buildings in 1874, is the site of the founding of the town of Spokane. By 1884, when this lithograph was drawn, Anthony M. Cannon was proprietor. (EWSHS)*

first to stake a claim on the north side of the river, a claim that included all the land around the present courthouse. The same year, W.C. Gray, a hotelier in Redding, California, came through to look and promptly bought the choice lot on the northeast corner of Front and Howard.

By 1880 "the Falls"—as most early residents called it—had a population of 350. Its streets were busier than that number would seem to warrant because homesteaders, prospectors, and other visitors came through daily. It was the dusty little Western town that forms the backdrop of hundreds of movies and novels of the Old West. A visitor that summer, if he had no personal conveyance, would arrive by stage. After an all-day journey up from Colfax in a cramped, swaying little car, he would jump down in front of the new stage and telegraph offices on the south side of Front Street. These buildings, like most of the buildings in town, were made of newly cut and unpainted pine. If the traveler asked the stage driver—wiry little Louis Yake, who carried both a bowie knife and a pistol in his belt—where there was a hotel, Louis would point to the corner across the street. The two-story building there had a fresh coat of paint and was made the more inviting by a wide, shaded porch

that ran all along the front and wrapped around the side. The hotel butted up against the river, and behind it, where Howard came to the river, the visitor would see a messy little backwater where logs and bark float together in the still water.

The California Hotel stood on the corner now occupied by the Carousel. Looking south from that corner, up Howard, one would see most of the town—three blocks of solidly packed wooden buildings. Signs on the big squared-off false fronts and on windows read "Jack Squire's Saloon," "McCammon and Whitman Men's Clothing," "R.W. Rima, Jeweler," "Graham's—Grocery, Liquors, Tobaccos."

In the whole town there were about fifty buildings, barely enough to keep the emptiness of the surrounding country at bay. Most of them were one story and cast little shade on the wide streets. The whole place baked under a hot sun.

The talk that summer and fall of 1880 was of two things: the arrival of the railroad from the west, which finally seemed

This 1884 view looks north from Howard Street and Front Avenue (now Spokane Falls Boulevard) toward Havermale Island. Spokane's first hotel, the California Hotel, stood to the east of the bridge. The Echo Roller Mills, built in 1883 and later owned by Albert Keats, utilized the river's power to grind flour, and was considered Spokane's most prominent building at that time. (EWSHS)

imminent, and the elections. Jimmy Glover and some other boosters had gone to Olympia and persuaded the legislature to create a new county out of a number of unwieldy counties that already existed. Spokane Falls had begun to take a leadership role in the region; its designation as county seat, to be formalized in an election that fall, would be its formal investiture.

But then there was trouble. About seventeen miles to the southwest, on the anticipated route of the Northern Pacific Railroad, there appeared some stacks of lumber, and then some frame buildings, and then a town, more or less. The new settlement announced it would call itself Cheney, after a Northern Pacific official. It also let it be known it would like to become the county seat. No one considered Cheney a serious contender in the county seat ballot until the town recruited to its cause a formidable editor in Colfax by the name of Lucien E. Kellogg. Kellogg hitched his presses to horses, like field artillery, and set out for Cheney. Having no building there, he set the presses up under a tree and began to bombard Spokane Falls. Kellogg reported that a Falls man had been overheard saying flatly his town didn't want the

business of farmers. "Farmers, [the story concluded] will you vote for Spokane Falls when it has told you it doesn't want your support?"

Spokane Times editor Francis Cook unlimbered his own guns and began to return in kind. "Cheney is a spot in the wilderness where an imaginary town exists," he reported to his readers after a visit there. Back and forth it went, in the two papers, along the roads, in bars, in farm-by-farm visits by emissaries of the two towns, until November 2, 1880, election day. The vote: Spokane Falls 563, Cheney, 680.

Spokane Falls was stunned. The bright future it had mapped out for itself seemed in danger. But the gloom was brief. The votes had to be certified by the auditor, and the auditor, a Falls man by the name of James M. Nosler, found that there were certain problems with votes from some of the precincts. He disqualified the votes of those precincts, and the result was to reverse the outcome of the election. Spokane Falls sent word to Cheney that it had lost after all.

Cheney swore all kinds of reprisals, but in the end only brought a lawsuit. The judgment was in Cheney's favor, and Spokane Falls was ordered to turn over

the county records forthwith.

History long ago decided, quite reasonably, that Spokane Falls had tried to steal the election (or at least steal it back, since Falls citizens believed that Cheney won only because railroad workers were transferred in by the Northern Pacific for the purpose of helping its chosen town on election day). Nosler himself maintained that he only ruled as the law said he must rule and didn't even know the outcome of the final vote until after his decision had been made.

The week of Cheney's victory in court there was a heavy snowfall that covered Spokane Falls to a depth of ten inches. James Nosler loaded his wife and two children aboard a large sled and they rode from their house east of town to spend an evening at Jimmy Glover's house.

Glover's little house stood next to the stagecoach office at Front and Howard. We can imagine the no-doubt distracted auditor being greeted at the door by the perennially jovial Glover. If we could just follow them into the parlor and listen to

their conversation that night, it is intriguing to think, we might learn more about these men and their motives in the election in one hour than we know after a hundred years. But history leaves us standing outside.

The most we ever get to tell us what these historic characters were really like is a kind of glance through the window—some little insight, perhaps from a letter or diary, that gives us a look at a real human being. It may be fragmentary but it is vivid—and it tells us things we never learned from documents and official statements. The letters of John J. Browne to his wife, for example, are filled with passages like: "This day perhaps has filled many a soul with joy and happiness, but I am lonely—my every thought is of you and darling little Guy. I hope you have kissed him, for me, many times today." After reading such passages the view one gets is unmistakably of the gentle-faced man with thinning hair hoisting and playing with his son.

There is no such view of Glover—the private man, as opposed to the ebullient founder contemporaries described. Glover never mentioned the wife who was undergoing the hardships with him. Local historian Jean Oton discovered why in court records of the era. Susan Glover was mentally ill. Police were often called to forcibly remove her from a stranger's house or yard. Glover, apparently estranged from Susan for some time, divorced her in 1892 and remarried the same year. Susan Glover was committed to Eastern State Hospital for the Insane at Medical Lake in 1899, where she died in 1922 and is buried. It was a peril of the stressful western experience pioneers seldom discussed.

We have a better view of the other man in the room that snowy night, auditor James Nosler. He began to keep a diary when he entered the Union Army in

Glover Block, one of the first brick buildings in Spokane, was built by James Glover in 1883. The building stood on the southwest corner of Howard Street and Front Avenue (now Spokane Falls Boulevard), directly across Howard Street from Glover's original trading post. (EWSHS)

1860 and it became a lifelong habit. The story it traces is twice valuable, both as the story of a single person, and as a story that is as typical of all pioneers as any individual's story is likely to be.

He emerged from the war determined to marry the girl he loved, though her parents were against it, and find his place in the world. He tried operating a general store in Iowa but soon concluded, as he said in his diary, "I can never stand this kind of do-nothing life." So he decided to try his luck out West. In 1870 he bought tickets on the just-completed Union Pacific Railroad to California and took his wife and three-year-old daughter, Flora, to the fabled West. That first night on the train, as he rolled toward the West, he wrote in his diary: "We are going to Oregon—not to find a Paradise, but a home among its mountains where Sallie can have better health and we can lay up something for the future, for the education of our children, and our own comfort should we live to become old."

He took his family from California to Oregon and then finally to Washington Territory, engaging in a number of occupations ranging from teaching school to lumbering and farming. But the dream didn't work as it was supposed to. Often his children went hungry. Settled in Colfax in 1877, he wrote in his diary, "It seems as though I can never make another raise. I have tried almost everything, but the mines. Verily the first thousand is harder to get than the next ten thousand."

That winter, in a passage that ran several pages of his diary, he described the death of the daughter he had brought West with him:

At 9 p.m. Dr. came over. After examining her he called Sallie out and told her that our little lamb would not live through the day. Her legs and hands and face were getting cold then ... She asked for her hoarhound candy and took a bite off of it. She then raised up by my assistance and looked at her Ma, who asked her if she saw her. She said yes. Her ma then asked her if she 'wanted to go and be with Aunt Ella.' She faintly whispered 'yes.' I asked her if she wanted to go and live with the angels. Again she whispered 'yes!' And just then I think the veil be-

tween her and heaven was removed. She looked upward with a look of wonderment and awe on her face and passed away without a struggle, only a few long breaths ... She died on my left arm and her ma holding her by the hand. Her last movement was to put her right hand to her head as though it itched ....

The next year, in October of 1878,

Nosler moved his family to Spokane Falls, becoming one of its earliest settlers. He homesteaded the property east of Division and south of the river, opened a land agent office, and built an office next to the California Hotel. He was in poor health. ("This morning I coughed up blood—the first time since that time in Oregon," he wrote in his diary February 17, 1879. "When there is anything the matter with me my great concern is for my family. I want to live as much to provide for them and get them in comfortable circumstances and beyond reach of want, as much as anything else.") Yet he became involved in a half a dozen enterprises in Spokane Falls, ranging from his real estate business to jobbing wood and contracting to build buildings. This was the man Spokane Falls appointed county auditor, and who ever since has been known to history only as "J.M. Nosler," the man who cheated Cheney in the county seat election.

Nosler's place in history was guaranteed a few months later. Spokane Falls citizens were moving slowly on the certification—perhaps hoping to hang on until it could be reasonably argued that a second vote should be held—so Cheney citizens, who lacked numbers but never nerve, took direct action. One night in March when nearly everybody in Spokane Falls was at a wedding party a group of Cheney volunteers walked quietly up Main Street. After a quick recount of the votes, with the aid of Nosler's successor, (Nosler had resigned), the Cheney men peremptorily declared Cheney the winner of the election, stacked the records on wagons, and took them home with them. The records, and thus the official county seat, remained in Cheney until the second election was held in 1886.

Spokane residents felt that the town's growth had been arrested by the loss of the county seat because many settlers

Below, left: *The clearing and grading crew for the first Northern Pacific Railroad through Spokane met this basalt outcropping just east of the present Amtrak depot at First Avenue and Bernard Street in 1881. It was one of the many obstacles the teams had to overcome in the Spokane area. The first train from the east came through the city in the summer of 1883. (EWSHS)*

Above: *This 1888 view of Spokane was taken at Pioneer Park, above Seventh Avenue looking north on Howard Street. The white two-story building two blocks down on the right is the Spokane School House, on the present site of Lewis & Clark High School. (EWSHS)*

Right: *When the city of Spokane decided to fund a college in 1881, Father Joseph Cataldo grew concerned about the strong Protestant influence in the area. Gonzaga was finally established by the Jesuits in 1887, and shown here in April of 1890. (EWSHS)*

Left: *The Comet Hose Team, also known as the Tigers, was Spokane Falls' first volunteer fire department, organized in the 1880s. This picture was taken on Mill Street (now Wall), along the east side of A.M. Cannon's Bank of Spokane Falls. A boy and dalmatian ride along as mascots for the team. (EWSHS)*

and businessmen chose to settle in Cheney. But that year of 1881 was nevertheless a signal one in Spokane's history. The city got its first brick building, the Wolverton on the corner of Riverside and Mill (Wall), and its first bridge, an island-hopping affair that started at the foot of Howard Street. And late that year the city of Spokane Falls was officially incorporated by the state legislature.

Most important of all, it was in the spring of 1881 that the Northern Pacific Railroad tracks were at long last completed through Spokane. Glover's little town was at last linked to the wider world. This link would be completed two years later when the western and eastern branches of the Northern Pacific met in Montana. After 1883 anyone in any Eastern city could be in Spokane in a matter of days, and in reasonable comfort. This spurred a tremendous boost in population. In 1888 alone over 1,000 people filed homestead claims for government-owned land in the Spokane Falls office.

Some people had warned Glover that the falls, though beautiful, might be a disadvantage to a city if the railroads considered them an obstacle. Luckily, Glover paid no attention, and just a few

years later these falls turned out to be an asset that no one could have anticipated. Even as Glover was founding his little city, Thomas Edison and others were perfecting the mechanisms for providing commercial electricity. When the technology was ready in the early 1880s, Spokane Falls found that it had a power source right in its midst. The town had electric street lights by 1886, making it one of the first electrified cities in the West.

The spring and summer of 1885 saw the discovery of the first two "hard rock" mines in the area—the Old Dominion a few miles from Colville and the fabulous Bunker Hill in the Coeur d'Alene Mountains. A stampede of gold-seekers fol-

Above: *Spokane Falls experienced a period of accelerated growth in 1887. This photo was taken from the top of Echo Mill, looking east and south. Havermale Island sits in the left foreground. The two-story structure on the near horizon is the first Sacred Heart Hospital. (EWSHS)*

Right: *Possibly the only photograph existing of the great Spokane fire of August 4, 1889, this view looks north on Howard Street from Railroad Avenue, about one block east of where the fire started. The street was cluttered with furniture and goods that had been cleared from the buildings that stood in the fire's path. (EWSHS)*

Right: *Workmen prepare to open the vault of James Glover's First National Bank, on the corner of Howard Street and Riverside Avenue. The vault was not opened until several days after the fire because of retained heat within the safe. Notice the armed guard standing in the ruins at left. (EWSHS)*

lowed, and mining would join agriculture in making Spokane Falls rich.

It was not, however, preordained that the wealth from the area's ore and grain be channeled through Spokane. While Spokane lay right between the great farmland and mining districts, it was by the same token close to neither. That disadvantage was neutralized by aggressive railroad building that soon made Spokane Falls the most convenient shipping point for thousands of farmers and tens of thousands of miners. Glover and several partners reached north with a railroad to the Okanogan mines. Cannon helped organize a railroad serving the farm towns of the Palouse. The newcomer Daniel C. Corbin pushed Spokane's influence eastward by building rails to the Coeur d'Alene mining district.

Now most of the business of this booming region would be channeled through Spokane. Between 1886 and 1889 the population of Spokane went from 3,500 to 20,000. Shacks, apartments, hotels and rooming houses sprung up in every vacant spot. Shops and offices expanded and proliferated to employ the newcomers. In 1889 Spokane Falls had six banks, twelve blacksmiths, fifteen barbers, four cigar factories, thirty groceries, ten lunch counters, sixteen restaurants and three theaters. The most widespread businesses were real estate offices (thirty) and saloons (forty).

Those quiet streets of 1880 now churned with life: cable and horse-drawn tramways plowed their way through the traffic; farmers loaded buckboards; sidewalks were crowded with miners, drifters, businessmen, Chinese, Indians (the famed Chief Joseph, assigned to the Colville Reservation after his defeat, was seen on these streets), messenger boys, prostitutes, shopkeepers, shoppers, and a constant parade of immigrants, satchels in hand.

A Sunday morning, particularly a hot, languorous one like August 4, 1889, would have been one of the few times things were quiet. Even the little flame that started up in a restaurant by the railroad depot seemed lazy. A man who saw it right after it started said a stream from a garden hose would have put it out easily.

But there was no stream forthcoming. The water that fed all the city's new fire hydrants (a matter of considerable pride) had been shut off, and the only man who seemed to know how to turn it on was out of town.

The flame grew, leapt across the street, took hold in a row of wooden buildings, then spread through the whole block. Some buildings were dynamited in an effort to cut the blaze off. When that had little effect, it became apparent that nothing was going to stop the blaze. The population, all except the two who died in the flames, escaped across the river or out into the fields. As night fell the fire was crested over the roofs of the city and shot burning timbers into the air like rockets. Only some quick dousings saved the buildings on the north side of the river.

The next day Spokane Falls was a twelve-square-block cinder. Some people hiked up the rail line and left by train forever. Slowly those who stayed moved in to explore: they found ragged brick walls and still-steaming telephone poles standing like ghosts in drifting smoke; a pile of black timber and metals at the middle of each lot; and little else except the acrid smell of roasted wood. James N. Glover had gone from youth to middle age building the city. Friday he and the other city builders had left desks piled high with plans and prospects. Now, Monday, they had no plans, no prospects—no desks! Everything that had occupied their minds for a decade had come to a halt as sudden and strange as death itself.

III

FORTUNES

Facing page: *Jacob "Dutch Jake" Goetz (standing on bottom step near banister) and his partner Harry Baer (to Goetz's left) posed with employees and customers in the lobby of their Coeur d'Alene Theater in 1894. As saloon owners in northern Idaho, Goetz and Baer provided a down-and-out Noah Kellogg with a small grubstake, in exchange for a portion of the prospector's findings. Jake's settlement from Kellogg's Bunker Hill strike alone ended up at nearly $200,000. The partners brought their money to Spokane, investing in this gambling hall at Trent Avenue and Howard Street. The establishment reportedly challenged "any fun place north of Denver," and included a variety theater, Turkish baths, dance hall, and food and liquor counters. (EWSHS)*

The gloom and shock of the fire were short-lived. Immediately those who had built the city took the lead in rebuilding it, and in the first year following the fire approximately 100 brick buildings were under construction in downtown Spokane. The city that was built over the next couple of years—buildings with red brick facades, studded with granite blocks and dignified by arched windows in upper stories—was the city Spokanites would know for the next eighty years, until the Expo '74 renewal. Traces of the old city are still there: in the "1889 Building" at the corner of Main and Stevens, the Bennett Block (1890) at Main and Howard, the Kuhn Building (1890), and the Review Building (1891).

In 1891, the city council shortened the city's name by dropping the "Falls." To draw the rapidly developing North Side into the city, the council ordered up no fewer than five new bridges that year, including a spindly Monroe Street Bridge on iron stilts.

Everyone was in an expansive mood. While the city constructed a new city hall (later to be razed for the railroad station on Front Avenue), white bricks from Clayton kilns were forming a fine French renaissance structure to house county government and courts. The cost of $376,000 was twice what the new city hall cost, and it raised some eyebrows. But it was a bargain, being that rare example of truly distinguished small-town civic architecture.

The boom of the mid-1880s had given the founders of the city some working capital and unlimited confidence that it would all happen again. Jimmy Glover took to wearing a top hat and built a mansion, Spokane's first, a rambling Tudor estate on the unsettled slope south of town. Anthony Cannon, of course, outdid that. He and John J. Browne ushered in Spokane's "Age of Elegance," as it has been called, by building the Auditorium, a cavernous theater draped in velvet and gold gilt.

The founders were able to rebuild in such style because among the farmers who had done well in the Palouse were some Dutch immigrants. These Dutchmen wrote home with praise for the potential of the land, but complained about 10 percent interest rates. Hearing about those rates and the demand, Dutch bankers sent representatives on the next boat with orders to loan whatever they could.

With the silver mines, agriculture, and trade all booming, investing in Spokane should have been the safe bet the Dutch thought it was. Then came what was known as the Panic of 1893. Around the world enthusiasm for buying and selling suddenly cooled. New York stock values collapsed and in nearly every town and village in the country people withdrew their money from banks to put it in a safe place.

Cannon's Marble Bank, having used a larger share of depositor's cash on ventures than any other in town, very quickly went under. News of this sent anyone in town who might have considered keeping a cool head running to the wire cages of all the other banks in town. Glover's First National Bank held on manfully for a few days and finally had to give up.

Right: *These brick-makers are from the J.T. Davie & Company brickyard, in 1890. The brickyard, located about three miles west of Spokane on Medical Lake Road, provided the brick for most of Spokane's buildings in the 1880s and 1890s. (EWSHS)*

Right below: *An 1890s view of Riverside Avenue looking west toward the intersection of Howard and Riverside. Courtesy, Northwest Room, Spokane Public Library*

Facing page top: *Dempsey's Restaurant on the southwest corner of Main and Howard in 1896. Courtesy, Northwest Room, Spokane Public Library*

Meanwhile, the Dutch bankers, themselves a little panicked, demanded immediate repayment of all loans. Since their cash had already been taken by depositors, one after another the Spokane bankers turned over their assets. Eventually a quarter of the city, incuding many of the major buildings on Riverside, was owned by a clutch of Dutch bankers on the other side of the world. To make the ill-fortune complete, a series of bad seasons in the 1890s bankrupted many of the early farmers of the area.

For the second time in four years the original city builders were wiped out. Some of them, the purposeful John J. Browne and the shrewd James Monaghan, for example, eventually recovered their fortunes. Glover became a civic elder, honored with directorships and a stint on the city council, but was never truly part of the city's top leadership again. He had lived in his mansion just months before he had to give it up to pay the bank's debts. Cannon left Spokane and traveled as far as South America looking for another stake so that he could begin again. In April of 1895 people back home got the word that he died alone and poor in a New York City hotel room.

That year also saw the death of Frank R. Moore, one of the original storekeep-

ers at Howard and Front along with Cannon and Glover. Like Cannon and Glover, Moore went into banking and like them he was ruined in the panic. He died of a painful stomach problem, at the age of forty-three, leaving his widow with a tangled mass of debts.

What was lost by some generally came into the possession of others, creating wholesale turnover in Spokane's leadership. The court-appointed receiver for

The Spokane County Courthouse Building, on Broadway between Jefferson and Madison streets, was constructed in 1894. The huge maple trees currently surrounding the courthouse are mere sprigs in this 1899 photograph, (EWSHS)

Frank Moore's affairs was F. Lewis Clark. Clark would handle the complex affairs masterfully, save the Last Chance Mine for the Moore estate, and in the process make himself a millionaire.

Clark was forerunner of a new leadership in Spokane. Harvard educated and financed by his banker father, he had come West in 1885, at the age of twenty-six, and opened a flour mill (the C and C Mill on Havermale Island) even as he strategically bought up real estate in the frontier city.

Daniel C. Corbin and the first William H. Cowles were of the same stripe. Corbin, whose mansion in Pioneer Park now belongs to the city, was older than most of the new wave of leaders, being fifty-seven when he arrived in Spokane in 1888. The face we see in photographs of him—trim beard around a firm mouth; strands of white hair laying across the pate like drifting smoke; unblinking eyes that stare back and seem to say "state your business and move on"—is a fair reflection of a flinty personality. If this was the "Inland Empire," here was the face of an emperor. Corbin was from an established New York family; a brother had built the railroad to Coney Island. But there was no family fortune, so Corbin had spent his whole life in the various enterprises required to develop a frontier.

In Spokane he pushed railroads out into the mining districts to tap for the city the wealth flowing from them. Then at the age of sixty-seven he became intrigued with the idea of making Spokane's agriculture bloom. He tried to establish the sugar beet industry here. It proved a costly flop, but led Corbin and a partner into pioneering one of the great success stories of the time: the irrigation of the Spokane Valley. He was thought a little zany for even trying, but by 1900 the first ditch was carrying water from Liberty Lake the six and a half miles to a farm dubbed "Green Acres."

Cowles had in common with Corbin his almost accidental appearance in Spokane. The *Review,* established in 1883 by a good newspaperman by the name of Frank Dallam, ended up in the hands of Harvey Scott, the opinionated and powerful publisher of Portland's *Oregonian.* That Spokane's major newspaper should be in the hands of a publisher from an enemy city—Portland was a competitor for dominance of the market to Spokane's southwest—was considered intolerable by many Spokanites. A group of them lured two *Chicago Tribune* journalists to Spokane to start another newspaper. They in turn, finding themselves with financial problems soon after starting the *Spokesman,* called in another partner—the first William Hutchinson Cowles. Aside from family money, Cowles brought to the enterprise the unusual combination of a Yale law degree and experience as a police reporter on the *Tribune.*

Meanwhile, Scott began to build a new headquarters, a red brick edifice with a higher steeple than that of the church it replaced at that corner. The cost of the

new building, the *Spokesman's* challenge, and the economic slump of the early 1890s soon had the *Review* under financial pressure. It was reportedly Scott's editor, N.W. Durham, who first approached Cowles and his partners about a merger to stop the murderous competition. The papers were combined, and soon thereafter everyone but Cowles seemed to lose their enthusiasm for Spokane journalism. Cowles bought them out. Five years later he purchased the *Chronicle* from John J. Browne and his partners and became the city's only publisher.

Much later, after World War I, Cowles would help maintain for Spokane its reputation as an extremely conservative community. But as a young publisher he was well out in front of the community's leadership on many issues. Under his leadership *The Spokesman-Review* urged liberal public expenditure on education, parks and public libraries, advocated a "windfall tax" on excessive earnings from land speculation, and endorsed the radical populist William Jennings Bryan for the presidency in 1896.

Of course, that endorsement of Bryan at least partly reflected the fact that Bryan's idea of allowing the unlimited coining of silver wasn't radical in Spokane. The city was quickly becoming the silver capital of the United States. The strikes of gold, silver and lead made in the 1880s were now, in the mid-1890s, being turned into huge mining operations with the help of Eastern seaboard capital. By 1896, the Bunker Hill, Sullivan, and a half dozen other mines in the Coeur d'Alene were producing 11,000 tons of silver-lead concentrates a month. That same year, the giant War Eagle and Le Roi mines just over the Canadian border in Rossland paid their first dividends to Spokane owners. Between 1895 and 1920, the mines of the area would produce well over one billion dollars in turn-of-the-

Left: *After he came to Spokane Falls in 1888, D.C. (Daniel Chase) Corbin started building railroads to the north and east. These railroads made possible the development of mines that later produced millions of dollars, much of which came to Spokane. Corbin's estate was estimated at over $12 million at the time of his death in 1918, and included the Cutter-built mansion overlooking the city above Seventh Avenue. (EWSHS)*

Facing page, top: *Building the Auditorium Theater was Anthony M. Cannon's most impressive achievement. Construction of the theater began in 1889 and was nearly completed before the great fire ruined what had been built. The reconstructed Auditorium was finally opened in 1892, and in the following decade it boasted the largest stage of any theater west of the Mississippi. (EWSHS)*

Facing page, bottom: *The opulent interior of the Auditorium Theater signaled Spokane's dawning "Age of Elegance." (EWSHS)*

Right: *Irish-born pioneer James Monaghan, seated at right, posed with his family for this portrait in the 1890s. Monaghan immigrated to the U.S. in 1856, and his shrewd investments made him rich. (EWSHS)*

Below: *Construction began in 1892 on what was to be the new home of A.M. Cannon's Bank of Spokane Falls. Unfortunately, Cannon never got the chance to move his bank into the new building, since his was the first to close its doors in the Panic of 1893. During the next sixty years the Marble Bank did house a number of financial institutions. (EWSHS)*

century dollars, and a good portion of it would stay in Spokane.

Spokane was to the mines what a theater headquarters is to the battlefield. Far removed from the blasting and daily assaults against the mountains, it was, nevertheless, where the generals gathered to lay their strategies. There were some 200 mining offices in the city at the turn of the century.

This is also where the miners came to escape the bleakness of the dusty mining camps. They congregated along the riverfront, where pool halls and hock shops were separated by dark and steamy saloons. Front Avenue alone had five large houses of ill repute. A little to the east, the area bounded by Howard, Bernard,

Front and Main, was called "Oriental Alley." Here, scattered liberally among laundries and other businesses operated by Chinese (who had been recruited to build the railroads, then cast aside), were opium dens and more houses of prostitution.

The best of the many gambling houses was Dutch Jake's, which by the mid-1890s was in its permanent home in the Coeur d'Alene Hotel (the building, now taller, still stands at the southeast corner of Howard and Spokane Falls Boulevard). It was four stories of big mirrors, long bars, good booze, green gambling tables, and glittering chandeliers. Cards were dealt by pretty women who wore tuxedo coats but no shirts, a costume that became a public issue, though the move to disallow it never succeeded. Jake himself was a good citizen and decent man who never turned away a cold or hungry human being.

Dutch Jake's was a public palace where miners in from poorly-lit and cold shacks could live like royalty for a few hours. Their employers, the owners of the mines, also came to Spokane to pursue

their fantasies. But they had no need for Dutch Jake's. Million-dollar gambles—buying and selling mines—were part of their daily business. And they could afford their own palaces, sumptuous mansions designed for them by a slightly built, quiet aesthete named Kirtland Cutter.

Cutter had intended to become an artist, an ambition which saved him from Yale, where his grandfather was a distinguished alumnus. Instead he briefly studied art in New York and London and then drifted through Europe making sketches of the landscape and buildings. A few years later he returned to the U.S. and traveled again, this time west. He arrived in Spokane in 1885, where an uncle was an officer in Jimmy Glover's bank. He brought with him a trunk full of fancy clothes and (for he was prematurely bald) a set of exchangeable toupees graduated in length to suggest growth. He worked briefly as a bank clerk and then went to work for an architect. Though he had no formal training in architecture, Jimmy Glover hired him to design his mansion. Cutter created a homey castle on the South Hill which established his

Left: *Pioneer miner Patrick "Patsy" Clark was born in Ireland on St. Patrick's Day in 1850. Clark ventured into the southwestern United States, where he started and operated several gold and copper mines. He migrated northward in the 1880s, working mines in Montana, British Columbia, northern Idaho, and Washington. (EWSHS)*

Below: *In 1890, the* Review *newspaper office was housed in this small wooden structure, on the southeast corner of Riverside Avenue and Monroe Street. The steepled First Presbyterian Church was torn down later that year, and replaced by the Review Tower in 1891. (EWSHS)*

reputation as Spokane's mansion builder.

Henry C. Bertelson, head draftsman for Cutter for fifteen years, said of his boss: "He never did any mechanical drawing nor did he ever use a square or a triangle. He carried a short, stubby pencil around in his shirt pocket [while on a building site] and when he had an idea he made his sketches."

In this way Cutter created, from his memories of European architecture, the buildings Spokane values most to this day. These include, to name a few examples, both Corbin homes and the F. Lewis Clark house on Seventh Avenue; the Graves and Davenport mansions on the north side of town (the latter is now part of St. George's school); and many of the most distinctive buildings downtown, including the Sherwood Building, the Catholic Diocesan headquarters, the Chronicle Building, and (his masterpiece) the Davenport Hotel. In each there is the beauty of conception and attention to detail that are the marks of art.

Cutter's designs provided Spokane's growing *nouveau riche* with instant heritage. Patsy Clark, for example, the tough

Irish immigrant who battled miners to a draw as manager of mines from Butte to Burke, and whose great renown stemmed from his stealing for Simeon Reed of Portland an advance sample of the Bunker Hill mine, could survey his own success as he stepped into the house Cutter fashioned for him on Coeur d'Alene Park. Cutter had made a trip around the world to pick out the materials and furnishings: bricks from St. Louis, the stained glass window and fixtures from Tiffany's of New York, the grandfather clock and other furniture from London, rugs from Turkey, and stonework from Italy. To paint the ceiling in the Louis XIV room he brought a muralist from France.

At the threshold of these mansions the dust and mud of the West gave way to new refinements. Wives who, like Mrs. Clark, had spent their first married years in rough mining camps, now planned elaborate formal parties and went calling on each other in their fancy buggies—a social custom for which a gaudy room just inside the front entrance was set aside. Evenings they would strap themselves into a body vise known as a whalebone corset for a performance at the Auditorium, thence to Davenport's Restaurant, where trout in big aquariums swam back and forth staring at diners.

A few blocks away from Patsy Clark's house Cutter was building, also in 1898, mansions for the biggest Northwest mining operators of all, the partners Finch and Campbell. For John Finch, Cutter designed a plantation-style mansion at the end of First Avenue, with imposing white columns and lawns spreading in every direction. For Amasa B. Campbell, Cutter created the solemn Tudor enclave that is now the county museum's best exhibit.

Visitors who inspect this mansion—its luminous Louis XIV sitting room, its ducal living room, its displays of fine China

Left: *Mine owner Amasa B. Campbell posed with his five-year-old daughter, Helen, in 1897. With John Finch, Campbell had extensive holdings in the Coeur d'Alene mountains, including the Hecla, Gem, and Kendall mines. Since 1925 Campbell's home, designed by Kirtland Cutter, has been known as the Grace Campbell Memorial Museum. (EWSHS)*

Below: *This view looks north on Howard Street, between Sprague and First avenues, in the 1890s. The Symons Building appears prominently on the right. (EWSHS)*

and the silk dresses—imagine an "Age of Elegance," as the era has been called. But much as the man who inhabited this model of an English gentleman's house might enjoy the role, Campbell was not a country gentleman. The mines attracted the ambitious, the smart, and the greedy from every corner of the country. Some innocents had stumbled into fortunes. But most could not depend upon luck. Campbell had lived in mining camps from Mexico to Alaska and was forty-five before he underwent the softening influences of wealth and marriage. He had lured his partner Finch and a handful of rich Ohio investors to the Coeur d'Alenes with promises of big returns, promises he was expected to keep.

Right: *On April 19, 1899, hundreds of disgruntled mine workers took control of the Bunker Hill Mine, at Wardner, Idaho, and planted explosives throughout the facility. (EWSHS)*

Right: *Colonel William H. Ridpath used his profits from the Le Roi Gold Mine to build an elegant hotel on First Avenue in 1899 between Howard and Stevens streets. The original Ridpath Hotel burned in 1950, but was rebuilt immediately on the same site. (EWSHS)*

Facing page, bottom: *This photograph of early Spokane mayors was taken in 1910. Pictured are: (Back row, left to right) Charles Fleming, Charles Fassett, C. Herbert Moore, W.J. Hindley, and (front row, left to right) David B. Fotheringham, James N. Glover, Daniel Drumheller, and Charles Clough. (EWSHS)*

In 1899, the year after the mansion was completed, Campbell was fighting refinery trusts trying to keep his ore out of the market on one hand, while he was dealing with miners constantly on the verge of rebellion on the other.

The rebellion came on April 29, 1899.

When the manager of the Bunker Hill Mine refused to give recognition to a union, a well-organized group of masked men hijacked a Northern Pacific train which was headed for the Bunker Hill. They used it to carry hundreds of armed men and dozens of boxes of dynamite to the mine. The men seized the mine with little trouble and stacked the dynamite inside the huge processing buildings at its mouth. Someone pushed a plunger and the buildings were reduced to slivers.

Campbell rushed to the Coeur d'Alenes to organize the defense of his own mines. He was armed and personally led a horseback chase of some of the outlaw miners. Only when he was sure things were under control in the mountains did he return to Spokane to organize a counterattack.

He figured the mines would be closed for a time. "I do not care," he wrote one of his partners, "this fight had to come."

Campbell and the other mine owners met and agreed to lock all strikers and sympathizers out and recruit all new employees. Campbell's partner, John Finch, was dispatched to San Francisco to begin recruiting workers. Meanwhile, at the goading of powerful mine owners, federal and state officials declared martial law in the mining district and rounded up hundreds of miners—mostly without proof that they had been a part of the assault on the Bunker Hill. The miners were kept in a makeshift prison at Wardner indiscriminantly and indefinitely—violation enough of basic rights even in those rough-and-tumble circumstances to prompt a Congressional investigation a year later.

The kind of power these mining lords could wield is suggested in a letter Campbell wrote to a partner in July:

... The Governor was up to Wallace with me and I read him your letter in regard to seeing the President. .. He informs me that he has already commenced corresponding with the administration to keep the soldiers there all next year at least, and he intends to continue martial law during his term of office. He intends that every man who ever belonged to the Miners' Union, and who was connected with these outrages, shall leave the country. The old sheriff and county commissioners have all been removed and we have a new set of county officials. The present board of county commissioners will see that no man gets a license to run a saloon in the country unless he can give excellent bonds and even in that case there will be very few saloons started. These places have always been the headquarters for plotting and nearly every saloon man in the country is an anarchist.

The deadly seriousness of the other side in this war was proven six years later when a man admitted that he had assassinated Idaho Governor Frank Steunenberg at the direction of the radical union leaders, who had sworn reprisal for Steunenberg's part in breaking the strike. But the victory of the mine owners came long before that sequel, and it was total, except that they often complained later that the replacement miners brought in

Left: *Colonel Isaac N. Peyton was one of three partners of the Le Roi Gold Mine to bring millions of dollars to Spokane. His Peyton Building was constructed in two considerably different styles. In 1898, the Great Eastern Building, on the southeast corner of Riverside Avenue and Post Street, was gutted by fire. Peyton bought the ruins, reinforced the shell, and added two floors. (EWSHS)*

to replace the strikers didn't work as hard.

The mines inevitably changed the character of a little inland town. Those who prospered from the mines by day stood askance at what the mines brought to Spokane streets at night. As the mayor reminded an overzealous police chief in 1897, Spokane was, after all, a mining town, and a certain amount of prostitution and gambling likely would have to be tolerated.

But most of the lasting changes brought by the mines were all to the good. Aside from the mansions, nearly all of which would come into public use, there was a tendency to invest mine earnings in local real estate. In 1898 a group of owners of the Le Roi mine over the Canadian border sold out to Canadian interests for three million dollars. Isaac N. Peyton used his share of the sale

to build on the corner of Riverside and Post, and his partner, W.M. Ridpath, invested in a hotel. A third partner, George Turner, the colorful U.S. Senator who sported a bushy black mustache, built the Columbia Building.

The great Hercules Mine, discovered in 1901, added a number of structures to Spokane's cityscape. August Paulsen was a young Swedish immigrant who drifted across the country in the 1890s. He found his way to Spokane, and from there to Burke, Idaho, where he took a job on a dairy farm. He met a young railroad engineer by the name of Levi Hutton and Hutton's betrothed, the operator of a Burke boarding house by the name of May Arkwright.

The three joined a half a dozen other equally poor friends to invest in a mine that had been abandoned earlier by savvy investors. They spent portions of their

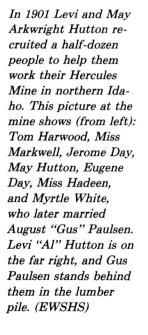

In 1901 Levi and May Arkwright Hutton recruited a half-dozen people to help them work their Hercules Mine in northern Idaho. This picture at the mine shows (from left): Tom Harwood, Miss Markwell, Jerome Day, May Hutton, Eugene Day, Miss Hadeen, and Myrtle White, who later married August "Gus" Paulsen. Levi "Al" Hutton is on the far right, and Gus Paulsen stands behind them in the lumber pile. (EWSHS)

The varied styles of turn-of-the-century Spokane architecture are vividly portrayed in this early 1910s view of Post Street at First Avenue, looking north. The elaborate clock tower at the near left is that of the Davenport Restaurant. The Auditorium Theater stands in the left background. The Peyton Building is a block down on the right. (EWSHS)

monthly salaries on dynamite and took turns working the mine. They kept it up for eight years with virtually no recompense. Then, in June of 1901, August Paulsen blasted away a curtain of rock in the mine and, when the dust settled, looked upon what proved to be one of the richest silver and lead finds in history, the famous Hercules.

Their partners, the Day brothers, would stay in mining and become one of the most powerful families in the history of Idaho. Paulsen and the Huttons would move to Spokane, each to leave a mark. Paulsen would immediately erect the first building that bears his name and plan the city's first "skyscraper," the Paulsen Medical-Dental Building (though he would die before he saw it finished in 1928). May, an outspoken woman who had a tendency to say "capitalist slave drivers" when she meant her fellow mine owners, went on to a fame independent of her money as a feminist and campaigner for women's suffrage. She and her husband were both orphans as children, and after her death in 1915 her husband created the famous Hutton Settlement a short distance outside Spokane. It was designed to give children without parents as normal a home setting as possible.

The Hercules would be the last major strike in the Coeur d'Alenes. Through the residuals of free-flowing gold, silver, and other treasures would last into the twenties, latecomers to Spokane would find that wealth, or even employment, was becoming difficult to come by.

But they continued to come looking nevertheless. Consider just one of these stories. In 1905 a young man who owned a small photographic shop in Lake Placid, New York, spotted a young woman in his shop and fell in love. Her father would not permit marriage unless the young man had more to offer than the security of a small shop. Specifically, the father said he would be impressed if, within one year, the young man could fulfill three conditions: (a) own a house, (b) have a bank account of $1,000, and (c) be earning $125 a month, a huge salary for that day.

A friend told the young man that Spokane was a likely place to begin, so he rode the train there and took a job as a salesman in the McGowen Brothers Hardware Store at Sprague and Wall. He worked twelve-hour days selling major hardware equipment and was soon making the required salary. After two years he had saved the $1,000 and had begun building a large house at S1115 Grand Avenue. He returned to New York, married the girl, brought her back to Spokane, and lived happily ever after as Henry J. Kaiser, one of the great industrialists of the twentieth century.

Spokane still had the touch.

IV

FRAGMENTS OF LIFE

Spokane had gone from frontier town to boom town to mining town to the gilded residence of millionaires in four quick decades. This burst of activity and wealth produced a city totally different from the Spokane of subsequent decades. Spokane had street lights before San Francisco and Portland. The Auditorium had the largest stage in the West outside of San Francisco and ranked as one of the finer theaters in the country. The Monroe Street Bridge was the longest concrete span in the country when it was completed in 1911, and the third longest in the world. For a few years in the early twenties Hollywood set up shop in Minnehaha Park and the beautiful actress Nell Shipman made a series of movies there.

Things happened during that period which are not likely to be repeated. The Davenport Hotel is the outstanding example. To produce such a building, Kirtland Cutter's talent and twenty years of experience building mansions, the perfectionism of Louis Davenport, and the availability of easy millions, all had to come together at a given time.

Davenport, who had already worked a small pancake house he started in 1889 into the city's finest restaurant, had the curious ambition of operating one of the nation's best hotels in Spokane. As unlikely as it seemed, the hotel he opened in 1914 achieved just that. A special plumbing system brought ice-cold drinking water to every room. The hotel's soda fountain made its own ice cream every day with imported chocolate and fresh strawberries. Employees were given a

course in the subtleties of "body language" (as it would be termed decades later) so they would not even unconsciously offend guests. In winter months the fireplace in the lobby was kept blazing around the clock, a job which required the nearly full-time work of a man on each shift. (It was in front of this fire between 1924 and 1929 that one could see Vachel Lindsay, one of America's best poets, sitting in a winged chair, enveloped in a creative daze. He had been lured to Spokane by a local admirer, and Davenport gave him the use of a large suite in the hotel at a bargain price).

Louis Davenport wrote articles on his philosophy of running a hotel and through them influenced the industry. Ernie Pyle, a nationally syndicated columnist in the 1930s and forties, was writing about a more famous hotel in 1939 when he said: "The St. Francis Hotel every night washed all the silver money it had taken in that day—did it in a whirling machine with washing powder and BB shot. The money came out looking as if it had just been minted. They said the idea originated at the Davenport Hotel in Spokane." In Louis Davenport, Kirtland Cutter (by this time known throughout the Northwest for his work) had found the perfect client, one who always put quality above cost.

Not all of the changes brought to Spokane by its surge of growth were beautiful. It was in this era that the river that had given the city its start was virtually lost to it. The city's railroad depot, Union Station, began to take over the riverfront in 1908. By the time it opened

Facing page: *Before the advent of self-service supermarkets, farmers from outlying areas brought their wares downtown to sell directly to the consumer. Horse-drawn wagons crowded together at the farmer's market, on the south side of Second Avenue between Stevens and Washington streets, in this circa 1910 photograph. (EWSHS)*

The Davenport Hotel, designed by architect Kirtland Cutter, attracted celebrities and royalty from the world over. The lobby's lavish decor included tropical plants, singing birds, and glass pillars filled with swimming fish. (EWSHS)

in 1914, a row of tracks, and later trestles raised on riveted black steel pillars, virtually sealed the city off from the river. Jimmy Glover's Front Avenue became the city's back entrance. The graceful Monroe Street Bridge was completed in 1911, but that same year it was marred by a shapeless rail bridge that passed directly over it to bring Union Pacific trains to Havermale Island.

Ugly though these changes may have been, the prominence of the railroads in the city was not out of proportion to their importance to it. Spokane had become a major railroad town, with five of the eight transcontinental railroads coming through the city. On a given day in the 1920s, over 100 trains would roll through the city. Little wonder that, to generations of children who lay in bed trying to sleep, the train's distant, unfolding wail was as familiar as the sound of rain on the window. The trains loaded and unloaded in Spokane twenty-four hours a day and then treaded their way

through hills, grass fields, along rivers and to lonely depots a block off the main street of some 500 little communities scattered around the region.

To a growing proportion of the passengers on those trains, Spokane was becoming just another of those lonely stopovers on the way to someplace else. At the turn of the century the Paulsens, Peytons,

Huttons and Ridpaths—Spokane owners of the great mines—began selling out to the John D. Rockefellers, J.P. Morgans and Jay Goulds, Easterners who would spend and invest their profits elsewhere. At the same time, towns in Idaho like Mullen and Wallace were growing enough to draw away some of the mining supply and entertainment functions Spokane had served. Mining money would always be important to Spokane, but after 1900 it would be split up many more ways.

That other indispensible client for Spokane's services, agriculture, was growing more productive all the time as steam and gasoline engines revolutionized wheat farming. Yet the odd economics of agriculture kept a lid on prosperity. Bad growing years hurt farmers, while good ones produced an oversupply which drove down prices and hurt them almost as much. World War I (which did little for Spokane directly, since most war supplies were produced in places where transportation was less of a problem) pushed up the prices of farm products. But with the end of the war, prices plunged again. A bushel of wheat that sold for $2.50 in 1918 sold for only ninety cents in 1922.

Spokane had been prevented from developing a larger manufacturing base by the price policies of the railroads. It cost

a Spokane business just about twice as much to ship raw goods from back East as it did a Seattle business, even though the Seattle goods had to travel even further. The difference was that the railroads had a monopoly in Spokane and other inland cities, while in coastal cities rail transport had to compete with ocean

Above: *Two days after the 1889 fire, Louis M. Davenport started "Davenport's Famous Waffle Foundry" in a tent with only 125 dollars. Within a year, Davenport was operating out of a new restaurant that would indeed become famous. In 1914, Davenport opened the three million dollar hotel that would bring the greatest fame to designer Kirtland Cutter. (EWSHS)*

Left: *When the third and present Monroe Street Bridge was constructed, it was the nation's longest and highest concrete span. (EWSHS)*

Above: *Sacred Heart, Spokane's first hospital, was a three-story brick building at the edge of the river, just east of the town center. It was the beginning of a tradition, as Sacred Heart and Deaconess hospitals made Spokane a medical center for an immense area covering four states and part of Canada. The hospital was rebuilt at Eighth Avenue and Browne Street in 1910, as shown here. (EWSHS)*

Right: *The Fox Theater, opened in 1931, was one of the last examples of fine Art Deco architecture in Spokane. The theater was the first built exclusively for moving pictures. (EWSHS)*

transport. The Interstate Commerce Commission, which had been lobbied for two decades by Spokane leaders, finally forced the railroads to standardize their rates in 1918. But in the meantime Spokane manufacturing, wholesaling, and retailing had developed under a heavy disadvantage.

All of these things took their toll, and in the second decade of the century Spokane had lost its status as a wealthy boomtown as suddenly as it had acquired it. By the time state prohibition shut Dutch Jake down in 1916 the excitement was over anyway, and he contentedly turned to serving malteds and colas to ladies and little girls at his bar. Kirtland Cutter finished up his plans for the Chronicle Building and moved to Southern California, where there was still money to build mansions. The Paulsen Medical-Dental Building (1928) was a final donation of the mines, and out-of-town money built the Fox Theater (1931). The emergence of a mass consumer market in the 1920s brought a new Montgomery Ward building and a new Sears Roebuck building in the summer of 1929 (eventually the former would become city hall and the latter the main branch of the public library). A population which had

soared from 37,000 at the turn of the century to 100,000 before World War I would grow only another 20,000 until World War II. In 1931, on the occasion of the city's fiftieth anniversary, the president of Whitman College tried to get the city's assembled leaders to imagine Spokane's bright future. "Perhaps it will shock you," he told them, "if I suggest that fifty years from now not one of the buildings which line your streets will be standing." What really would have shocked them would have been if the speaker had guessed that forty years later *all* the same buildings would still be standing; that for four decades there would be almost no improvements to Spokane's downtown area.

In most books, pamphlets, articles, and dissertations about Spokane's past, the final passages describe the sale of the big mines and history draws to a close about 1920. Of course, to people who lived in Spokane in the subsequent decades it didn't seem that way. Life—real, everyday life—went on.

History has a pattern, that checkerboard of events and intertwining causes which we study to extract lessons. Like the pattern in a quilt, it is what we see when we stand off at some distance and

Above: *The Great Northern Railroad was the first to lay track along the Spokane riverfront and Havermale Island, in 1901. By the time this picture was taken, in 1924, the railroads had overrun the island and south bank. (EWSHS)*

Above, left: *The soil of the hills to the south and west of Spokane would prove to be the most enduring source of wealth for the Inland Empire, but clearing it of bunch grass and bringing in those early crops was arduous work. This circa 1915 picture was taken on the farm of John A. Fancher, a pioneer who settled near Deep Creek southwest of Spokane in the 1870s. (EWSHS)*

Above: *The Spokane-Coeur d'Alene interurban electric railway made regular stops at Liberty Lake starting in 1910. By the summer of 1913, special trains were leaving Spokane every few minutes to bring thousands of swimmers, bathers, and picnickers to the most popular of the area's lakes. (EWSHS)*

Right: *A popular turn-of-the-century outing included an interurban train ride to Coeur d'Alene, followed by a steamboat excursion around the lake and up the St. Joe River. (EWSHS)*

Left: *Ingersall's Park, a large field at the west end of Boone Avenue, was a popular picnic and baseball spot for Spokanites as early as the mid-1880s. In 1909 Washington Water Power converted it into the Natatorium Park amusement area as an incentive for riders to use its Monroe-Boone railway line. Some of the later attractions of Nat Park included the "Jack Rabbit" rollercoaster, the airplane ride, "Dodg'em" bumper cars, and the famous merry-go-round. It has been estimated that over four million people rode the merry-go-round while at Nat Park. In 1967 the Nat Park amusements were dismantled to make way for the San Souci West Mobile Park. The merry-go-round is now preserved at Riverfront Park. (EWSHS)*

These kids in the 1920s are getting a thrill on the "Jack Rabbit." (EWSHS)

Bobsledders enjoy the steepness of Howard Street near Seventh Avenue, in the winter of 1890-1891. The large building in the right background is the Spokesman-Review Building before its tower was added the following year. (EWSHS)

look. But history also has a texture: the way it actually felt to those who touched it. Unfortunately museums cannot preserve, alongside their fragments of history—letters, weapons, clothing, utensils—these fragments of life: the feeling of a favorite coat to a particular woman on a particular evening in her life; the back yard on a warm summer afternoon as experienced by a twelve-year-old boy or girl. For most people most of the time, these evanescent moments are what the past really was. One's hometown, by providing the weather, the sounds, the diversions, the tempo of life, has much to do with fixing this texture.

What constituted the texture of life in Spokane? Surely the lakes were an important part of it. Roger Anderson, a city councilman in the 1970s who had moved to Spokane from the west side of the

state, once observed that when he first arrived he was puzzled to hear people say they were going to "the lake," as if there were only one. The Spokane expression—which refers to lakes as a universally understood experience rather than a specific place—suggests the role played by the seventy-six lakes within commuting distance of Spokane. By 1902 electric trains were leaving Spokane daily to take people all the way to Lake Coeur d'Alene. In the opposite direction, little Medical Lake enjoyed a sudden popularity when it was supposed that the murky water had curative powers. A full-fledged resort drew hundreds of swimmers on a weekend.

Liberty Lake, being the nearest at hand, was the most popular at the turn of the century and through the 1920s. Developers built a resort hotel and a dance hall on pilings out over the water. When the sun finally went down on a summer night, fireworks often lit up the sky and a steamboat pulled a floating dance floor around the lake. By 1911, trains on Sundays and holidays would deliver five cars full of picnickers every hour. Every company, school, lodge and nationality had its annual picnic, with fried chicken, watermelon, soda and kegs of beer. The biggest crowd ever recorded at Liberty was that of July 4, 1924, when an estimated 14,000 people stepped over each other trying to get to the water.

About that time automobiles and better highways began dispersing the crowds to more lakes. But the essential experience of the lake—long summer days, the sun hanging motionless in the sky, the drone of voices on the water, the rattle of the diving board and the sound of the plunge—would remain the same in 1980 as it was in 1940 and 1920 and even 1902.

Almost as redolent with memory, at least to anyone who was born prior to 1950 or so, was Natatorium Park, a strange assortment of mammoth machinery arranged along the lower Spokane River for the purpose of selling thrills to the crowds which swarmed its lawns and pathways on sunny afternoons. It was constructed in 1887 as an incentive to use the new cable line that traveled to it via west Boone Avenue. Rides were added every year—the Tunnel of Love, the Shoot-the-Shoots, the Jack Rabbit—until it became the major diversion of pre-television decades. Its finest piece by far was the merry-go-round, carved in hardwood by the now famous Charles I. Looff of New York City. It came to Spokane in 1911 as part of a deal that allowed Looff's new son-in-law to become a partner in the amusement park. When the park was closed in the 1960s, the merry-go-round (now called the Carousel) was saved and eventually re-erected in Riverfront Park.

As the city's first park board president and "civic development" writer for the Spokesman-Review, Aubrey L. White campaigned twenty-six years to beautify the city and develop parks. White was responsible for securing the undeveloped land for Riverside State Park, Mt. Spokane State Park, and Deep Creek Canyon, to name a few. (EWSHS)

The three decades following 1920 were the era of the park. Manito Park, which housed the city zoo until it was closed in 1933, drew visitors from all over the city by way of the trolley that rattled and clanged its way up Grand Boulevard. It was almost as popular in winter as in summer because of its sledding hills and large skating pond. Most parks in the city had skating ponds in the winter, even if they were only tennis courts flooded by the city park department. In contention with a day at the lake for the most common association with "growing up in Spokane" would be one of white landscapes and blue winter evenings, the muffled click of ice skates, the vague scent of wood and coal smoke mingling in the fresh cold air.

Spokane acquired its national award-winning park system largely through the personal efforts of a man by the name of Aubrey L. White. White had come to Spokane from Maine in 1889 at the age of twenty. He was sent back East in 1896 to sell mining stocks in New York City, and there for ten years he viewed first-

Above: *This photo of the Musicaladers appeared in an advertisement for Lareida's Dance Pavilion in the Spokane Valley. Courtesy, George Lareida, Jr.*

Right: *"Field Day" attracted hundreds of spectators to the quarter-mile horse and bicycle track at Corbin Park, near Cleveland Avenue and Howard Street. People all over Spokane hopped onto streetcars to come to Corbin Park for a day of band concerts, leisurely walks, and the races. (EWSHS)*

hand both what an urban area can be like without parks and the complications of trying to create parks after an area has already been developed.

When he returned to Spokane to find it booming and headed for exactly those same problems, White organized his powerful mining acquaintances behind a campaign to change the city charter. His aim was to set up a park board independent of the city council. The charter amendment passed, and White became the reconstituted park board's first president in 1907. His first action was to hire as consultants the Olmsted brothers of Massachusetts, designers of dozens of urban park systems, including New York City's Central Park.

The report prepared by the Olmsteds was bold. Even as Union Station was being constructed, the report pointed out what a mistake it was to spoil the river's natural beauty like this. The report also said Spokane needed five times as much park space as it had.

The Olmsted recommendations became Aubrey White's marching orders. He laid the city map before him and concocted strategies to take prize pieces of land, along the river and throughout the city. When he ran into serious obstacles he would gather a select group of backers—William H. Cowles, Sr., John Finch, Louis Davenport and Joel Ferris—for a luncheon and a solicitation. What was not donated one way or another was purchased with part of a one-million-dollar bond issue White got voters to approve in 1910. By the time White left the park board in 1921 most of the city's park system had been assembled.

A small fraction of the work White did for Spokane was leading the park board to plant 80,000 trees along its streets, and encouraging citizens to add more. His friend and supporter, millionaire developer Jay P. Graves, planted the trees along Grand Boulevard. Among the trees planted under White's supervision between 1910 and 1920 are the very ones that still

Above: *Many Spokane couples danced across this floor at Whitehead's Dance Palace in the 1920s. (EWSHS)*

Above left: *The young Bing Crosby often came to Whitehead's on West 313 Sprague Avenue to listen to the music of the Jazz Age. (EWSHS)*

shade Riverside Avenue west of Monroe, Mission Avenue, and numerous other streets.

Behind those trees were built, from about 1900 to 1930, the big, bulky family houses of Spokane's close-in neighborhoods. Visitors often find these well-preserved neighborhoods—ranging from the stately homes opposite the Cheney Cowles Museum to the plain, box-like houses of Peaceful Valley just over the bluff—the most fascinating part of Spokane.

It's entirely appropriate that it was a Spokane woman, Mrs. John Bruce Dodd, who in 1910 originated the observance of Father's Day. This is when Spokane was making the radical transition from boomtown to "a nice place to raise a family." That was the reason that Harry Lowe Crosby gave for moving his family from Tacoma to Spokane in 1906. The most remarkable thing about Bing Crosby's childhood in Spokane is that there was so little remarkable about it. He swam at Mission pool, delivered the *Spokesman-Review,* loved playing baseball and pranks, got in the requisite number of fistfights, and couldn't sing all that well. He was the typical Spokane kid. The family, mom and dad and seven children, lived in a big yellow house at E508 Sharp, one block from the entrance to Gonzaga University. Bing attended Webster Grade School and Gonzaga High School before he entered Gonzaga's law school. He had dreams of becoming a great trial lawyer, but those apparently bogged down amid the profusely footnoted statutes.

The talent that everyone who knew Bing in Spokane remembers is not his singing but his witty tongue. George Lareida, who hired Crosby's band, has said that when you see him in the "Road" pictures trading quips with Bob Hope, "that's the fellow he was." Arthur Dussault, S.J., a chum of Bing's, remembers working out with the Gonzaga basketball team while Bing, typically, provided from the sidelines an unsolicited, needling, but funny commentary on the action.

When Bing started performing, it was as a second-rate drummer in a band that did mostly instrumentals. The band, called the Musicaladers, booked minor dances and restaurants around town. None of its members had much musical training. They built up a repertoire by going to Baily's record store near the northwest corner of Riverside and Post and crowding into the booths to listen to a record over and over until each band member had his part memorized.

The winter of 1925-1926 they played at Lareida's, a former automobile display room on the 4900 block of East Sprague which had been transformed into a popular dance hall. On a bandstand in the middle of the floor, sitting behind a bass drum decorated with a Japanese painting of a sunset, hundreds of Spokanites of the "Jazz Age" saw Crosby perform over the winter of 1925 and 1926. The Musicaladers had to be inventive to fill a whole evening with the few songs they were able to memorize. They would take a waltz and play it as a foxtrot, or copy the Dixieland style. At intervals Bing would step forward for some somber lowing about losing the one you loved, or with a livelier tune of the day.

That spring Bing and Al Rinker, the talented piano player who had started the Musicaladers, landed a job doing musical warm-ups to silent movies at what was then known as the Clemmer Theater (now the State Theater), at the corner of Sprague and Lincoln. Here they began to polish the little act—Rinker at the piano singing along as Bing warbled and joked through a brief medley of songs—that would take them both to fame a few years later.

After the show Bing usually went to

When Norma Talmadge and the cast of "Smiling Through" posed in front of the Liberty Theater in the early 1920s, downtown Spokane had no less than fifteen theaters. The Liberty, located at West 716 Riverside Avenue, was considered the downtown picture house, competing with the Clemmer, until the Fox was built in 1931. The Liberty seated 1,000 people, and is credited with running the first sound movies in town. The theater was remodeled into Lerner's Dress Shop in 1953. (EWSHS)

Stubeck's confectionery, on the northwest corner of Sprague and Wall, a hangout for young people of that time, or up the street to Whitehead's dance hall where he could listen to other bands play. This was the major gathering place during Spokane's roaring twenties.

It was outside Whitehead's that Dutch Groshoff, a friend of Bing's and a well-known Spokane musician, came upon Bing about midnight one night. Bing, still dressed in his striped jacket and bowler hat, was handcuffed to a policeman who was arresting him for possessing bootleg liquor. As the policeman requested a paddy wagon from a nearby callbox, a small crowd from the dance hall gathered and appealed to the cop to let Bing go "this time." When the paddy wagon arrived, the policeman opened the rear doors, climbed in, and pulled Bing up after him. As Bing stepped up, he turned, doffed his bowler hat with his free hand, and executed a grand bow to the crowd. The policeman jerked the handcuffs and Bing disappeared into the dark wagon.

Later that spring Father Dussault found Bing in a vacant lot behind the Crosby house and across the street from Gonzaga tinkering with an ancient automobile. Bing told him he and Rinker had purchased the car and were going to use

it to blow this burg—go to the big time. That was a familiar refrain among Spokane kids in these decades when there was little economic growth to provide jobs for all the children growing up in the large families of the era. Dussault advised Bing to at least finish out the semester of law school—just in case he didn't become a big Hollywood star.

On the appointed morning Rinker showed up at the Crosby house and was amazed to find Bing still slumbering peacefully. The two loaded Bing's drums in the back of the old car, said goodbye to the Crosby family, and pulled away from the curb. They drove down to Stitz' gas station at Boone and Division, where a friend gave them a fill-up and agreed to catch them later for the money. Then Bing put the flivver into gear and started south on Division.

Anyone who turned to look at them pass by would have witnessed an historic moment: Bing Crosby on the road to Hollywood. Or so it seems to us now, in retrospect, with the whole pattern of his subsequent success in place. At the time it was just another few moments of "now," another fragment of life. To a couple of Spokane boys putt-putting toward the Division Street Bridge on a brisk spring morning it was just "today."

V

THE WIDE WORLD IMPINGES

A person sitting down with a cup of coffee and the *Spokesman-Review* the morning of October 24, 1929 would have the future in front of him, if only he could know how to decipher the hints. A cartoon on the front page joked that railroad service was soon going to decline to the point where people would find it easier to take a bus, or even an *airplane!* Page two of that morning's paper told the reader: "Theoretically, it is possible to transmit the image of a man making a speech, while the radio carries the voice. Ultimately, you may be able to sit beside your receiving set and watch a football game in progress while the announcer gives the running account of the game." A few pages further on, an editorial noted the continuing squabbles between France and Germany and was thankful that President Wilson had not been able to get the United States in the League of Nations at the end of World War I.

But the big headline of that day read: "Cataclysm Hits Stocks In Hour . . . Prices Flatten Out Like Punctured Balloon." If the reader was an investor in the stock market, as millions of ordinary people were in 1929, he had to be concerned. But no matter how shocked our reader, he could hardly have suspected, as he finished his coffee and stepped outside to a clear, 65-degree day, that everything was about to change. Whatever he had planned for the future, and whatever the community had planned for its future, it was all changed now. For the next sixteen years Spokane was at the mercy of larger forces, like a cardboard box tossed and flipped in a hurricane.

The effects of the stock market crash and ensuing economic chaos were gradual but relentless. The city's loss of economic momentum is reflected in the steady fall of the value of the construction undertaken. From $4.1 million in 1929, Spokane building permits fell to $3.6 million in 1930, $2 million in 1931, and finally bottomed out at the standstill level of $572,000 in 1932.

The Farmers and Merchants Bank closed in November of 1931, and the Wall Street, State and American Banks closed a few months later. Rumors swirled around the fate of the Old National Bank, the epitome of financial security and holder of one out of four accounts in the region. It closed with the national "bank holiday" on March 2, 1933 and didn't reopen until October 9 of that year, at which time depositors were allowed to claim up to 40 percent of their deposits.

Spending during Christmas of 1932 was half what it had been three years earlier. Two large department stores, Culbertsons and the Palace, were among the dozens of businesses which collapsed under the financial pressures. At the depth of the Depression in 1932, only one in seven street-level addresses along Riverside were vacant. But one in four of them had either been under new ownership since 1929 or were completely new businesses.

Unable to collect property taxes, city government cut its 1932 budget by 20 percent. One of the things cut was the zoo in Manito Park. The parks director could not even give away the animals to another city, so several of them, includ-

Facing page: *Newsboys like E.A. Cahill, shown here in 1924, shouted out the day's headlines each evening as people headed for the trolley and their Model Ts. The newsboys' chants were a part of the fabric of life in the 1920s and 1930s. (EWSHS)*

The Lincoln Statue, sculpted by Alfonzo Victor Lewis of Seattle, was dedicated November 11, 1930, at a spot about thirty feet south of its present position. Films of the dedication show a time capsule placed in the base of this statue. Although there is no record of its contents, the capsule would surely reflect the last moments of innocence in Spokane. (EWSHS)

ing two grizzly bears and a polar bear, were killed and stuffed to be placed in the city's museum.

Approximately one out of four of all Spokane workers were without jobs, including many who headed families. Very few could get county relief money, so they borrowed or they simply went hungry. Others jumped aboard railroad trains and began to drift from place to place, as people all over the country were doing. Boxcars draped with hundreds of people—men, women and children—were a common sight in Spokane. So many drifters arrived in Spokane that the city government established a transient hotel that could house up to 600 people a day. These transients were allowed to stay up

to thirty days and then were forced to leave town.

Dr. Alexander Barclay of Coeur d' Alene abolished all debts owed him for Christmas of 1932, saying, "I believe that this should be done generally, as far as possible, all along the line, if people are to retain their courage to continue to battle for their homes and families. The suicide list is growing appallingly and the spectres of debt, want and misery are stalking the land with Seven League Boots. Peace on earth, good will to men."

The emergency relief programs of the Roosevelt administration began to take hold early in 1934. That year the heads of 6,000 Spokane families received federal paychecks. They were paid for their civic

This aerial view of the downtown business district was taken in 1931. While the valley and surrounding areas would undergo drastic expansion, downtown Spokane would change little in the next thirty-five years. (EWSHS)

C.E. Marr established the first self-service grocery store in Spokane in 1918. Prior to the opening of Marr's Store Number Two on Riverside Avenue, east of Lincoln Street, shoppers read a grocery list to a store clerk, who ran back and forth plucking the items from the shelves. By 1921 there would be thirty "Marr's Help Yourself Stores" in Spokane and they would be a familiar part of daily life in every part of town. Marr's grocery chain eventually evolved into Piggly-Wiggly's and Safeway. (EWSHS)

work and, though the purpose was to feed families, the city got some important work done in these years at bargain prices. Crews on federal relief payrolls put in fifty-five miles of sewers, virtually completing the city system. Others grad-

ed streets, rebuilt the Felts Field airport and renovated many of the city's schools. White collar workers did everything from indexing the local newspapers to teaching night classes offered free to the public. Crews of the Civilian Conservation Corps, a federal program that brought young men here from all over the country, built many of the campgrounds and roads still in use in forested areas of the region.

One of the largest of all Roosevelt programs, and in fact one of the largest construction programs in the history of the world, was proceeding just seventy-five miles west of Spokane. Grand Coulee Dam would change the history of the state and Spokane by irrigating tens of thousands of acres of land and making industrial and private energy cheaper in Spokane than in any other place in the country.

Partly as a result of federal programs, the economy began to recover quickly af-

President Franklin D. Roosevelt, flanked by his sons John and James and Washington Senator Clarence C. Dill, left, waved good-bye as his train left the Ephata Great Northern station, following his first visit to the Grand Coulee Dam site, August 7, 1934. The construction of Grand Coulee Dam, for decades the world's largest dam, changed Northwest history by using inexpensive power to draw aluminum and other industries, and by irrigating thousands of acres of previously dry farmland. Senator Dill, a Spokanite, was an early Roosevelt supporter, and was instrumental in winning presidential support for the Columbia River project. (EWSHS)

ter 1937. By Christmas of 1939, spending in downtown department stores finally returned to what it had been in 1929. Seven days later the Depression decade was happily forgotten in parties at the Davenport Hotel, Spokane Club, and many other places around the city.

To many people and in varying degrees, the thirties had been idle, drab, impoverishing, humiliating, and horrible. The first half of the coming decade would prove frenetic, vivid, prosperous, glorious—and to many equally horrible.

December 7, 1941 was a sunny winter day in Spokane, with temperatures in the forties. Many people heard the news of the bombing of Pearl Harbor on their car radios as they drove home from church that morning. Others stopped what they were doing at home and turned the radio up loud to listen to the reports. Many people remember getting phone calls from excited relatives. What did it mean?

It was one of those rare times in life when every single person in a community had a clear sense that his or her life was going to change.

In the days immediately following Pearl Harbor, lines formed at local recruiting stations and the Armory was swamped by enlistees and draftees lining up for physicals. John Matsch, forty-two years old and a veteran of World War I, was at the recruiting office December 8, 1941, trying to get back into the Navy. He finally wrangled his way in six months later on the basis of his technical skills from the last war. In the process, one of the recruiters he had badgered said, "Why don't you just wait? This thing is going to last a long time and we'll come looking for you sooner or later." It was a long war. Toward the end men in their late thirties and men with several children were being fitted for uniforms so that they could replace the teenagers who had gone in the beginning.

Approximately 15,000 people from Spokane County were in the armed forces during World War II. Ask anyone born before about 1925 where he or she was on a given date between 1942 and 1945 and you are as likely to hear "Burma" or "Tarawa," "Salerno," "Normandy" or "Berlin" as you are "Spokane." It was as if the city had shattered with Pearl Harbor, scattering its pieces to every corner of the earth.

Dozens of Spokane men were killed or taken captive in the initial Japanese attacks on Pacific islands. Among them were Sammy Gracio, the pilot who would become the city's first hero by escaping from a prisoner of war camp, and Lloyd Catlow, a Marine who was one of the last Corregidor holdouts to be captured.

Spokane was the home of two major reserve units at the outset of the war. The 161st Infantry Regiment of the Washington National Guard, which drew rifle companies from throughout eastern Washington, would fight through Okinawa and Luzon and eventually take part in the occupation of Japan.

The 14th Marine Corps Reserve battalion, also based in Spokane, was called into active service a year before the outset of the war. The unit was divided up and its members scattered throughout the Pacific.

Among them were six boyhood friends who had enlisted in the unit together in 1938: Jack Burke of Gonzaga High School; Bill Higgins of Lewis and Clark High School; Oliver Hauschild of North Central High; Bud Womble of Rogers; Ray Morse of North Central; and Phil Baldwin of North Central. Their fates are a snapshot of the war in the Pacific. Burke was a bombardier on a torpedo plane and was killed shortly after Pearl Harbor when his plane went down in the Pacific. Higgins was taken prisoner by the Japanese at Guam. Hauschild and Womble were both wounded at Guadalcanal, the first step in the American counter-offensive. Morse was one of the defenders of Midway when the Japanese were thwarted in their attempt to invade by the sudden arrival of the Amer-

ican fleet. Baldwin was one of the 4,500 Americans killed at Iwo Jima at the doorstep of Japan in 1945.

In the first year of the war defense installations began to fringe the city like modern ramparts. This was a war of *materiel,* and Spokane shipped off hundreds of thousands of tons of it. To the north and east of the city (separated in case of a bombing attack) were the federal government's aluminum mills. Also in the valley was the Velox Naval Supply Depot, opened January 1, 1943. In its twenty-nine large warehouses (which would become the Spokane Industrial Park after the war) it stored: 110,000 galvanized buckets; 2,500 sixty-man life rafts; 137,000 hospital blankets; 7 million bottles of insect repellent; 660,000 pounds of medicated cotton; 300 train carloads of Navy clothing; and countless other items which would have to be disbursed around the world before the war was won.

To the city's southwest was a much larger operation, the Army Air Corps supply and repair depot known as Galena. It was one of four such installations in the country and had been vigorously courted by the Chamber of Commerce in the years just prior to the war. Galena served as a kind of giant pit stop for bombers. A damaged or worn plane would land on its criss-crossing airstrips and head for a cavernous hangar that covered eleven acres of ground. In a period of three or four days, crews working around the clock would have gone over every rivet and bolt, in essence turning out a new plane. In its two years of operation more than 10,000 airplane engines were repaired at the depot.

At the city's west gate was the venerable Fort George Wright. Just prior to the outbreak of World War II it had exchanged the last of its old army mules and horses for mechanized transportation. For awhile it was an Air Corps headquarters—the one to which Lieutenant Clark Gable reported on January 10, 1943. (The star of *Gone With The Wind,* which premiered at the Fox Theater April 18, 1940, was a distraction because secretaries all over the post kept finding excuses to go through his office). Toward the end of the war the fort became a convalescent hospital.

To the northwest of the city (on the site of the present Veterans Hospital) was Baxter Army Hospital. The injured came to it in caravans from all over the world. On one particular day it admitted 256 patients; by May 5, 1945—two days prior to victory in Europe and three months before victory in Japan—it had logged 10,000 patients.

The mood of the city was combative. No matter what the losses suffered by Americans, newspaper stories always took a "you should have seen the other guy" slant. People returning from the front were interviewed, sent to high school convocations and paraded through downtown. A big military parade on July 22, 1944, had appropriately attired clowns with signs around their necks reading "Adolf," "Benito" and "Tojo" being pulled along by ropes around their necks.

In one sense there were few places on the face of the earth more remote from the war than Spokane. But in another sense every battle cast its shadows across the city. At the sight of a Western Union boy riding down the street, people would drop what they were doing and hold their breath; if he stopped, their lives might change forever.

When her nineteen-year-old son got his wings in the Army Air Corps, Mrs. Helen Mangan, the wife of a Spokane police sergeant, wrote a poem:

Dear God, it seems but yesterday
you gave this son to me.
The one who's miles from
home
Whose face I cannot see.

The years have swiftly come and gone,
So eager in their stride
To brush me lightly by the way,
And take him from my side.
It seems to me he's still a child. . .

He was killed one year later when his B-17 was shot down in France. Alan Campbell Powell, grandson of Amasa B. Campbell, a bomber pilot as well, was also killed in France. Cheney Cowles, the second son of the *Spokesman-Review* publisher, was killed in a plane crash in the states while training. Captain Jack Miller, the thirty-year-old Princeton-educated grandson of Spokane pioneer and millionaire Patrick Welch, died in the

During the Second World War it was not uncommon to look down a Spokane street and see more people in uniform than in civilian dress. This photo was snapped toward the end of the war, looking east down Sprague Avenue from Lincoln Street. Courtesy, Spokane Magazine

Although every house-hold in the nation was affected to some degree by the war effort, few Spokane-area families suffered more loss than the Bangs. Melvin, Peter, Irene, Sidnie, and John Bang all left their Spokane Valley home to join the armed forces. Melvin and Sidnie died overseas. On this page, clockwise, are Melvin, Irene, and John. Facing page, left to right, are Peter and Sidnie. Courtesy, the Bang family

Soloman Islands. Archie Buckley, the popular head football coach of North Central, was trying to help another man during an attack on their aircraft carrier when he was killed. Private Joe E. Mann of Reardan, after parachuting into the Netherlands in September 1944, was wounded two different times, once in each arm, during fierce close-in fighting. A grenade landed near him but behind other members of the platoon in the bun-

ker. With both arms bandaged to his sides he was unable to throw it, so he yelled to the others and then covered the grenade with his body just as it exploded. He was awarded the Medal of Honor posthumously.

With approximately 15,000 people from Spokane County serving, virtually every family had someone to worry about. Few families had more on the line than the Bang family, which had immigrated from Norway to the Spokane Valley in 1921. Five of eight children were in the service: Sidnie was on a tank destroyer in Europe, John was on a ship in the Pacific, Peter was with the Army in India, Melvin was in the Army Engineers in the Pacific, and Irene was in the Waves in California. Sidnie is buried in Belgium and Melvin is buried in the Philippines.

In all, there were about 500 who did not return to homes in Spokane and the Valley.

It was about 4 p.m. on August 14, a Tuesday, when Spokane got the news that the war was over. As word spread downtown by radio and word-of-mouth, people came streaming out of department

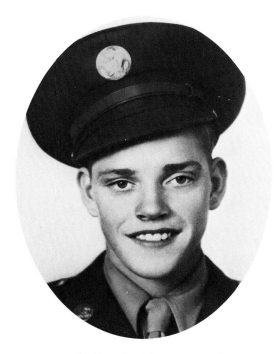 

stores and office buildings onto the streets. "For the first few minutes there was little noise," the *Spokesman-Review* reported. "Then automobile horns began to blow. In a few minutes their blasts became a solid wave of sound in downtown streets."

In those first few moments of knowing it was all over a person could hardly do otherwise than review what the war had meant: loneliness; people who would now be coming back; people who wouldn't; friends in foreign lands and tropic jungles; going home. All sorts of emotions exploded on the crowded downtown streets. Next to people laughing and embracing were people crying and being comforted by strangers. Instead of subsiding, the celebration intensified late into the night until downtown streets were clogged by bumper-to-bumper cars and the sidewalks were impassable.

Of course, the end of the war came differently to many other Spokanites. At the northern edge of Japan, in a place so remote that vehicles could not reach it, an American soldier arrived by parachute to tell Sergeant Lloyd Catlow, a Marine

captured on Corregidor, and about 200 other American prisoners the news—which they had already guessed when their Japanese guards had suddenly disappeared. Food was dropped in for the following three weeks so the half-starved men, most of whom had been in the deadly camps three years, could build up the strength to walk out.

Catlow returned to Seattle by British and American ships. From there he had the choice of returning to Spokane by train or bus. He chose the bus because he had been thinking for weeks about what it would be like to come down Sunset Hill again and see Spokane. "I had that imprinted on my mind," Catlow remembered later. "I wanted to look down on the city from Sunset Hill." Late one afternoon in the winter of 1945 the bus rolled over the West Plains, reached the crest of the hill, and started down. Catlow leaned close to the bus window and looked. "And there she was, spread out at the bottom of the hill, just like I imagined it."

For many people, the war was over the day they got home.

VI

SPOKANE RECUMBENT

Spokane emerged from the war with a revitalized economy. The twin aluminum plants at Mead and Trentwood were purchased from the federal government by ex-Spokanite Henry J. Kaiser and began supplying the modern metal to civilian markets. The Army Air Depot (renamed Fairchild Air Force Base in 1950) became a permanent installation and added a huge military payroll to the city's economy. The Navy's abandoned Velox Supply Depot, with its neat rows of warehouses on railroad sidings, supplied ready-made housing for dozens of new businesses as the Spokane Industrial Park. Geiger Field, the landing strip begun by the city just prior to the war and completed by the Army Air Corps, was now turned back to the city and Spokane had a modern airport. Each of these new assets produced its offshoots: construction of houses, new businesses (an example was the new fabricators of aluminum products), new stores, and restaurants. Very few of the 10,000 discharged GIs returning to Spokane had trouble finding jobs.

The GI Bill and no-down-payment terms meant almost anyone could buy a house. In 1947 alone there were 2,500 houses built in Spokane, five times as many as any year prior to the war. Fields of wild grass and basalt outcroppings at the north edge of the city were suddenly covered with pastel houses and lawns nursed by hissing sprinklers.

Nineteen-fifty-five was a good year for city housing, with over 2,800 lots platted. But that same year there were twice as many lots platted beyond the city's lim-

its, most of them to the east in the Valley. It wasn't noticed yet, but the city was undergoing profound changes.

After World War II, the faster automobile, improved roads, and cheap gasoline made it possible for the middle class to combine the prosperity and diversions of the city with the pastoral quiet of the country. And land "in the country" was often cheaper than city lots. This and the fact that one did not have to pay for sidewalks, sewers, police protection, and many other expenses of urban life usually made up for the cost of fuel for the commute back and forth.

Bigger populations in the Spokane Valley, which set up demands for better roads (culminating in the completion of the I-90 freeway in 1967), drew still more people to the valley. Meanwhile, the city taxpayer bore the whole cost of maintaining an expensive city core, even though that core was used just as much by many Valley residents. The difference in tax burdens became one more reason to move beyond the city limits.

All of these things set up a kind of centrifugal force that was pulling population, particularly younger and more affluent families, from the city and scattering it about the surrounding environs. In 1940, the Spokane Valley was mostly orchards and small farms and had a total population of 10,000. By 1960 that had increased to 45,000, and by 1970 to 60,000—the population of a medium-sized city.

This separation of the city from a large portion of its population was the cause of two of the most serious crises in Spo-

Facing page: *Spokane of the 1950s was made up of turn-of-the-century buildings modified to meet the needs of a half-century later. The photo shows Bennett Block and Dutch Jake's Coeur d'Alene Hotel. (EWSHS)*

Riverside Avenue in the early 1950s. The photo was taken from the Spokesman-Review Building tower. Courtesy, The Spokesman-Review

kane's history. The first was the threat to health when an urban area grew up without the standard urban sewer system. The explosive growth in the valley was nominally under the direction of the government of Spokane County. But a board of three commissioners, formed by the state constitution in the last century mainly to oversee the maintenance of roads and other minor services required by a rural area, was ill-equipped to deal with the complexities of urban development. Essential services like water supply and fire protection were provided by independent districts. But certain things—

overall planning for example—cannot be done piecemeal. Neither the traditions of county government nor the personalities of those usually elected to serve in it provided the impetus to take hold of the fast-changing situation.

Among the consequences was that the valley became one of the largest urban areas in the country not served by sewers. The rocky valley soil and substrata happened to be almost perfect for the septic drain field system of sewage disposal. Sewage virtually never saturated the soil and appeared on the surface of the ground, the kind of failure which

In the early 1920s, Spokane citizens authorized the expenditure of $1 million to build a coliseum, but a debate over where it should be located delayed, and then ultimately scuttled the idea. The issue was revived after World War II by a group of citizens who put on a successful campaign to finance a coliseum. The 8,000-seat Coliseum, at Boone Avenue and Howard Street, was completed in 1954. Prior to its construction no indoor theater or arena in town would hold more than 1,000 people. (EWSHS)

usually forced a town to begin the expensive process of installing sewers. Unfortunately, the same permeability which allows sewage to move so reliably downward is, at a deeper level, what allows water from mountains and lakes of Idaho to flow underground to Spokane, supplying the city's drinking water. If the two—the valley sewage and the water in the underground aquifer—should begin to mingle, one of the finest natural water supply systems in the world would be tainted.

In the early 1960s a consultant told the county that pollutants probably were not reaching the aquifer. In the early seventies new studies indicated they probably were. But in the early 1980s the county took the first steps toward building a valley sewer system. Presumably the city's irreplaceable water supply finally would be safeguarded.

The second threat of the postwar move to the suburbs was to Spokane's downtown. The people who now found shopping at a nearby shopping center much more convenient were the same people who had been supporting downtown restaurants, theaters, and other attractions. The loss of the retail shopper had made many American city centers compounds

of business and professional offices which on a weekend showed hardly a sign of life, something not quite a city, something perfectly described by Gertrude Stein when she said of Oakland: "There's no *there* there."

In Spokane this nationwide trend toward the desertion of the city core was one more burden in a time of general decline. After the initial boom of World War II and the years immediately following, the city's economy began to slide again. In one disastrous year (1957), the wood products industry went into a slump, Kaiser Aluminum reduced its operations, and the Air Force moved units of fighter planes from their base at Geiger Field. Many other businesses and regional offices were closed about this time, and one study indicated that between 1957 and 1963 the city had lost six percent of its jobs. A study of the fifties and early sixties by Gonzaga University said: "The Spokane economy, contrary to bright reports in the local media, was not making very great progress. In fact our data indicated that Spokane was nearly standing still relative to itself and was falling behind in comparison to other areas."

The city's malaise was apparent every-

The Parkade is a landmark of Spokane's renaissance. Its construction in 1966 was the beginning of the city's decade of downtown renewal. The second-floor skywalk was initiated with the Parkade. The first skywalks, shown here, were arched concrete walkways with plastic-covered canopies. The alley behind the Parkade and Fidelity Bank Building was converted into an open plaza. (EWSHS)

where. Many downtown addresses were vacant. The public face of the city, its city hall, was a weary, clanking six-story building with the general demeanor of a jailhouse. Perhaps the perfect symbol of neglect was the condition of the city's major physical attraction and distinction, the river. Though the state director of health had certified the Spokane River as a health hazard in 1935, it was still being used as an open sewer twenty-five years later. Spokane did not have a sewage treatment plant in operation until 1960, long after Pasco, Ellensberg, Walla Walla, and many much smaller communities had working systems.

In the late 1960s a national writer by the name of Neal R. Pierce toured the Western states and wrote an overview called *The Pacific States of America* (1972). Pierce saw Spokane like this:

Physically, Spokane is like warmed-over 1930s except for one very modern parking garage. Two railway lines slice right through the middle of town. The city is terribly ingrown, insular by definition, and has historically been dominated by the most reactionary business groups (especially mining and the railroads). Seattle people hold Spokane in unkind contempt; one told me, 'If you could just move a couple thousand interesting people into Spokane, it would be a pretty fine place to live.' A Seattle economist in 1969 referred to Spokane as a place 'with no real growth elements, even though it has tried to lift itself by its bootstraps with a reasonably successful industrial park.'

One is tempted to say that when you ask Seattlites what Spokane is like you learn mainly what Seattlites are like. In fact, the same writer added to the above passage: "As Seattle slid into deep recession in 1970-1971, Spokane's more diversified agriculture-mining-manufacturing economy continued to hum, raising the question about whom the last laugh might be on." But this ducks a truth even Spokanites were recognizing in the early 1960s. The city had some fundamental problems and was not progressing as it should.

What the cause of this might be was the subject of a great deal of study in the mid-1960s. Dr. Henry Kass, a political scientist at Eastern Washington University who specialized in local government, pointed out in a contemporary study that Spokane was a city of low personal incomes yet high home ownership, meaning it had many "marginal homeowners"—people who had little money to spare after paying the expenses of home ownership and other living expenses. Getting people to tax themselves more for major urban improvements was bound to be an uphill battle, particularly since bond issues required a 60-percent majority to pass.

But even taking this into account, Spokane was an extremely conservative community. Kass compared Spokane with twenty-two other cities about the same size and found that eighteen of them allocated a greater portion of their total incomes to roads, sewers, public buildings and other capital expenditures that upgrade a city. One explanation is that the biggest taxpayers of all were downtown property owners, and in Spokane these property owners had a great deal to say about what the city could or could not afford.

Since the days of Glover and Cannon, Spokane had been a city driven not by political comers, aristocracy, bosses, or absentee millionaires, but by businessmen who worked a full day in their offices and watched events in the city along with all the other variables that might affect business. They owned Spokane—or at least the heart of it, its central business district—and were therefore responsible for it in a way not even the passing political leader could be. They were executives of the major banks and department stores, as well as owners of other downtown buildings, top executives of the Washington Water Power Company, and newspaper publishers. On many matters before the city they had no group interest. But when they did, they could exert powerful influence—as respected opinion leaders, officers in many civic and charitable organizations, as employers of a large portion of the city's population, as lenders, lessors, and in many other ways.

Charles Olmstead, another Eastern Washington University political scientist, writing in the same EWU report as Kass, said: "The size of Spokane, the stability of its population, the close-knit nature of its business and professional world have 'personalized' political and social differences of opinion. The costs of speaking out have often been the heavy ones of personal animosity and sanctions." That no doubt puts too harsh a light on the situation. The city's leadership in these years might be seen as a close-knit, like-minded family which could not understand when someone wanted to rock the boat—and certainly could not allow them to do so. The same group cohesion did a lot of good things. A member of this group could—and often did—pick up the phone and in twenty minutes of calling around town collect any amount of money for a charity or other cause.

The analogy with a close-knit family

The merry-go-round and bumper cars of Natatorium Park continued to thrill Spokane youngsters into the 1950s and 1960s. (EWSHS)

came near to being true because of many intermarriages among Spokane's top families. There were perhaps two dozen key families in Spokane's establishment from approximately 1925 to 1960. By virtue of its longevity and high profile, the Cowles family was in the popular mind the one "that runs Spokane." If not quite equal to that myth, its dual ties to the business community and, through the newspapers, to public opinion, made it immensely influential. Orville C. Pratt, superintendent of Spokane's public schools in the twenties and thirties and an able chronicler of its history, said of the first William Cowles: "In all probability no other citizen of Spokane has had as much influence in determining the sort of city (Spokane) has become. Personally, Cowles was modest, self-effacing, quiet, upright, likeable and inflexible . . . It is open to question whether any one man should be in a position to wield such great influence, although with Cowles it was in safe, though conservative hands."

The official history of the *Spokesman-Review, News For An Empire* by Ralph E. Dyar, enumerates the paper's many crusades: for the city's charter change in 1910; against a bonus for World War I veterans; for strong enforcement of Prohibition laws; against local corruption; for many community charities; against rate-setting practices by the railroads that gave coastal cities better rates than Spokane. "A characteristic feature of *The Spokesman-Review's* campaigns in these and other instances," the book says, "was that they were not confined to the columns of the paper. They might include conferences; a war chest; mobilization of public-spirited citizens; speeches before organizations; the appointment of some one person to take charge of a certain campaign; the preparation, printing, and distribution of pamphlets and circulars; the financing of a delegation to go to Washington, D.C., to bring pressure to bear on the lawmakers in the interest of the community; and other missionary work."

That kind of onslaught for the public good was admirable. But what is for the "public good" is not always obvious, and Cowles, as a major property owner downtown, had a built-in conflict of interest. In 1935, the federal government wanted to finance a two million dollar sewage treatment plant for the city under the Works Progress Administration. Because the city would be required to put up the estimated $20,000 a year needed to operate the plant, the project came in for a fierce bombardment on the *Spokesman-Review's* front pages. The first of the articles (December 2, 1935) ran under triple-decked headlines: "Sewage Scheme Causes Alarm . . . Plan Voters Rejected Would Mean Big Cost Yearly . . . No Health Aid." The story that followed did not quote federal officials about why they were putting the proposal forward, nor the city commissioners about why they might be considering accepting it. Instead, the front page story was a mixture of personal opinion and quotations of others with like opinions:

The WPA's proposed sewage disposal plant gift to the city [the December 2 story began] is one gift horse that is being looked in the mouth by the recipients . . . . The issue is whether the city has any need for the plant, and if so, whether its value is sufficient that the city should incur a minimum annual charge of $25,000 to keep it working. The state board of health has investigated pollution of the Spokane River, and has found that it is not sufficient to be a nuisance . . . . Even if there were cities below Spokane, there would be no health menace, because the Spokane River is sufficiently large and swift to carry off the sewage and purify it . . . . Chief advocates of adding the new sewage disposal tax to

Spokane's expenses are fishermen, who say that if the dumping of sewage into the river stops, there will be good fishing. For $25,000 to $80,000 a year the fishing ought to be extraordinary. . . .

Granted it was another era, one in which publishers felt freer to use their publications for personal advocacy. But this and the other stories in the series were remarkable for totally ignoring every other point of view and even the facts. One would never guess that the state director of health had said two years earlier that Spokane needed a sewage treatment plant "for public health purposes." The state director of health's annual report for that very year, 1935, listed ten rivers in the state in which sewage was a problem. The Spokane River was the first listed and the only one characterized as "grossly polluted" rather than just polluted. The idea that rivers and streams automatically purified themselves, stated as fact in the story, was a popular misapprehension state health authorities were trying to clear up at the time. But no public health authority was quoted in the stories. All the opinions cited were those of Spokane businessmen.

If the voice in the *Spokesman-Review* suggested a curmudgeon, people who knew the senior Cowles found him personally courtly and considerate. He died in 1946 at the age of eighty. Under his son, William, Jr., the *Spokesman-Review* and *Chronicle* became gradually less conservative.

It was not the opposition of the Cowles, nor the parsimony of marginal homeowners, which kept the city from completing so fundamental a public utility as a sewage system for so long—until 1960. *The Spokesman-Review* gave up its opposition in the 1940s and Spokane citizens voted a $1.7 million bond issue to finance a treatment plant in 1946. The state pitched in another one million dollars for the plant—and added an order to the city to quit pouring its sewage into the river. But the city's governing body, the Board of Commissioners, decided in 1948 to reject all the bids for construction of the plant on the grounds that costs of materials may go down later. The five commissioners took the action squabbling, as usual, and there was some suspicion that individual commissioners wanted to use the treatment plant money for more immediate pet projects.

One of the obstacles Spokane had to deal with in the postwar years was its government. In 1910, citizens had adopted the commissioner form of government, which was then considered to offer the ultimate in efficient and responsive urban management. Each elected official would directly manage a group of city departments, so there would never be any question about who was responsible for what. If the roads were bad a citizen could vote against the commissioner of public works; if the police were corrupt the resident could vote against the commissioner of public safety. That was the theory.

In practice, the responsiveness of the commissioners could get out of hand. Since each commissioner made his reputation by redressing complaints against the services he was in charge of delivering, he had no incentive to give up anything in his departments for the larger good. At the same time, a general election is not necessarily the best way to choose a person to oversee the day-to-day details of running a street department or fire department. Instead of responsiveness and efficiency, the commissioner form of government became identified with squabbling and ineptness.

By the mid-1950s, two civic action groups, the Municipal League and the League of Women Voters, had concluded that Spokane should consider changing to the city manager form of government. As the commissioner form of government had been the rage among reformers a half century earlier, now the city manager form, modeled on the management of private corporations, was seen as the way to straighten out city hall. The city manager was a non-political specialist hired to make the city machinery run smoothly and cheaply. He was under the general direction of a kind of "board of directors," a "weak" mayor and council which would set policy but have absolutely no management powers.

Thus, the alternative had already been identified when dissatisfaction with the commissioners finally exploded into revolution. The cause of revolt was the imposition by commissioners of a tax on gross incomes of businesses (a business and occupations, or B&O, tax). With the economy in a slump in the late 1950s, few people liked the idea of a new tax, but to business in particular a B&O tax was anathema. A local advertising man by the name of Charles Devine, always described in the newspapers as representing unnamed "prominent businessmen," announced in November of 1959 that there would be a petition drive aimed at changing the form of government. The Municipal League and the League of Women Voters joined the campaign, and by January of 1960 enough signatures had been gathered to put the matter on a March ballot.

The commissioners responded with a series of actions and statements which at once made them look like men desperately trying to preserve their jobs and made it clear why the government should be changed. Rather than defend the commissioner form, the commissioners suggested that they might put another item on the ballot calling for a change to the *strong* mayor form of government. It was interpreted as an attempt to confuse the issue and led to a series of stormy confrontations between citizens and commis-

sioners. Police and firefighter unions added to the confusion and controversy by collecting money and campaigning to retain the commissioner form of government while at the same time picketing city hall for higher wages. Finally, with the election nearing, four of the commissioners came out of a secret meeting and announced that they had stripped Gaines Sutherlin of the title of mayor (which was bestowed by a vote of the commission) and had named in his place Kenneth Lawson, the one commissioner who had been criticizing just about everything the other commissioners had done for years. Lawson's elevation to mayor could only be interpreted as an admission that things had been about as bad as he had been insinuating all those years.

On March 8, 1960, almost exactly fifty years after adoption of the commissioner form, voters replaced it with a city manager and seven part-time council members. The vote was 30,107 for the change and 19,970 against it.

The following June seven city council members were elected, all but one of them businessmen. The new mayor was Neal R. Fosseen, a vice president of the Old National Bank and the epitome of Spokane's civic/business leaders. Some people had opposed the new form of government on the grounds that it would be less responsive to the general citizenry and more responsive to business—a theory about city manager systems political theorists generally accept. But in the years following the change-over there were no drastic changes in the direction of city services (according to a study by Dr. Kass), except that they became more efficient. In the meantime, Spokane's business community had in effect accepted official responsibility for making the city work. This would be a key to the phenomenal era about to get under way in Spokane.

The years between 1945 and 1960 were

hard-working ones. Dozens of small businesses were started and had to be fanned to life with all the more vigor because of the economic chill. When the people who went to work at Kaiser Aluminum in the late forties began retiring thirty years later, the company suffered a noticeable drop in productivity. Many of those same people were building, evenings and weekends, thousands of new homes added to the city in these years, and most were engaged in rearing the post-war "baby-boom" generation.

The question is, why didn't all this energy translate into civic progress? A city planner by the name of King Cole noticed something about the city when he first arrived in 1963. Its citizens were almost routinely disparaging of it. People referred to the city as "Spokaloo" and "Sin City"—the latter an ironic suggestion that there was nothing to do. The man who installed Cole's telephone said, "You're moving *into* Spokane? I'm getting out as soon as I can." A clerk at the local Payless Store, chatting as she put his purchases in a sack, said, "People are moving out of this city in droves." Charles Olmstead, one of those political scientists scrutinizing Spokane in the mid-sixties, said at the time: "The most pervasive and important attitudinal fact about Spokane is its serious lack of self-awareness . . . The city is unclear as to why it exists, where it is going, and how it will get there."

Thus, as Spokane entered the 1960s, it had a long list of chores to tend to: revive the economy, refurbish the downtown, replace city hall and the airport, and clean up a river still being polluted because the just-opened sewage treatment plant was inadequate. But an even deeper problem was a lack of that pride-in-ownership, that sense of community, which could persuade residents to tend to the city's civic tasks.

Railroad yards, warehouses, and parking lots dominated Havermale and Cannon islands and the Spokane riverfront in this 1966 aerial view. Within the next eight years the area would undergo rapid change, the only remnant of the railroad age being the Great Northern depot tower. (EWSHS)

VII

"THE EARTH DOES NOT
BELONG TO MAN,
MAN BELONGS
TO THE EARTH"

SPOKANE RESURGENT

In 1958, Joe Kipper, then president of the Spokane Chamber of Commerce, called an informal meeting of the thirty or so people who owned and managed downtown Spokane. Those gathering in the board room of the original Seattle First National Building at Riverside and Howard included the managers of the department stores, shops and hotels, representatives of all the banks, descendants of mining millionaires Peyton and Paulsen, William Hyde of the Cowles Publishing Company, John Hieber, manager of a large portion of the downtown properties, and Kinsey Robinson of Washington Water Power Company.

What Kipper had to say that day was basically: "If you guys don't wake up you're going to lose your downtown."

To many sitting in the room things did not look so dour. In the last few years, Spokane's downtown had received a new Newberry's store (1952), a new Penney's (1953), an addition to the Crescent (1956), and the Bon Marche store (1957). But Kipper, as manager of the local Sears store, had the perspective of a chain that kept in touch with what was happening nationwide, and what was happening nationwide was that suburban shopping centers were draining the life out of traditional urban centers.

As a result of Kipper's meeting, several of those present formed an organization called Spokane Unlimited to begin planning for the future of the downtown area. The new organization hired a New York urban planning firm called Ebasco Services to draw up a master plan. The so-called "Ebasco Plan," unveiled in 1961, envisioned a huge pedestrian mall replac-

ing automobile traffic on Riverside; six square blocks at the east edge of the central business district devoted to new government buildings and spacious lawns; and a riverfront cleared of railroads and adapted for "cultural uses."

Voters were asked in March of 1962 to launch this ambitious plan by approving a $10.5 million bond issue to build a new city hall and establish the governmental center envisioned in the plan. They said no, and by a huge margin. The results were about the same two years later when a slightly less expensive proposal was put on the ballot. The typical Spokanite did not identify with a "beautified" downtown area. For decades downtown property owners had treated the heart of the city as their own personal business. Now they had made a plan to renovate it without consulting citizens. The voter's attitude was clearly, "pay for it yourself."

Nevertheless, citizens could not just tend to their neighborhoods and ignore what was going on downtown. The city would inevitably be judged by this half-mile-square section, and a vital downtown was Spokane's best chance of improving its entertainment and cultural life. Most of all, the falls was a place of natural beauty which begged to be returned to the whole city. These kinds of considerations spread concern for the city's center beyond the business community. By the mid-1950s "riverfront renewal" was a major topic of conversation at club breakfasts and over private lunches. City Planner Vaughn Call began to hold public hearings in the early sixties on what then seemed impossibly futuristic

Facing page: *Fireworks burst above the United States Pavilion during Expo '74. The U.S. Pavilion theme "Man and Nature: One and Indivisible" was expressed by the quote seen at the pavilion entrance. The words featured on the wall are those of a Northwest Indian chief who rebuked a delegation of white settlers who wanted to buy his land more than a century ago. (EWSHS)*

Riverside Avenue in the 1950s. All three department stores that are visible, Newberries, Crescent, and Grants, eventually went out of business as suburban malls began to open around the city. Courtesy The Spokesman-Review

plans for a riverfront returned to public use.

To get things moving, the city council tried to get aid through new federal programs which financed urban renewal. But many Spokane citizens were suspicious of strings attached to federal funds, and the debate over seeking federal money consumed much of the energy that went into city politics through the sixties. Those opposed to Spokane's participation in federal programs always won. One more potential avenue toward recovery was blocked.

Spokane Unlimited, too, was groping. In 1963 it hired as its first full-time director King Cole, an affable, articulate attorney-turned-city-planner who had helped San Leandro, California, renovate

its downtown and dock area. Many people at Spokane Unlimited were surprised when Cole's first action was to help form a broad-based citizen action group called Associations for a Better Community (ABC). The purpose of the organization, which was made up not of individuals but of representatives of 195 other organizations in the city, was to begin the process of forming a concensus about the community's overall goals.

The following year, 1965, Cole attended a conference in St. Louis, a city which had replaced center-city train tracks and trestles with a park. St. Louis had done it, Cole learned, by getting the National Park Service to stage an exhibition on the site and therefore foot most of the bill for reclaiming the area. Cole returned home and immediately tried to interest the U.S. Park Service in sponsoring some sort of exhibition in Spokane, a city with closer access to more national parks than any other in the country. He got nowhere, but the idea of an exhibition as a catalyst was established.

It was about this time residents began noticing that the city had centennials approaching (whether the proper date to be observed should be 1871, when the first settlers came; 1873, when the first permanent settler came; or 1881, when the city was chartered, was a matter of preference). Cole suggested Spokane Unlimited sieze the opportunity and sponsor an exhibition tied to Spokane's centennial. On his advice Spokane Unlimited hired Economic Research Associates (ERA) of Los Angeles to evaluate the possibility.

The Los Angeles organization reported back that the regional birthday party just wouldn't generate the kind of money needed to produce important changes in the city. Then it made the suggestion that changed Spokane's history. Why not, said the investigators, go all the way and hold a world's fair? The consultants provided a theme, ecology (for this was the emerging concern of the time), and had even taken the liberty of checking with the Bureau of International Exhibitions in Paris and found that there were no conflicting fairs scheduled in the early seventies.

On the basis of ERA's figures and the personal enthusiasm of King Cole, the Spokane Unlimited-sponsored "Spokane Centennial Committee" voted, in late 1970, to change its name to the Expo Corporation. Cole became general manager. The summer of 1974 was chosen because it could be done no earlier, and a later date would clash with celebrations of the nation's bicentennial in 1976.

As simple as that, Spokane had committed itself to producing a world's fair by May 4, 1974. Only gradually, as the

requirements of such an undertaking began to take shape over the next couple of years, did people realize what they had gotten themselves into. A world's fair is a colossal undertaking, even for a larger city with lots of capital to draw on. Spokane had the minimum amount of time to put a fair together—and could not even start until it dealt with the sticky problem of moving three railroads. And the Spokane River was still quite polluted because of Spokane's inadequate sewage treatment plant and dozens of polluters upstream as far as the mines of Idaho. Did Spokane dare invite the world to come to talk about ecology on a site that overlooked a polluted river? Two of the city's oldest and most formidable problems—reclaiming the river from the railroads and cleaning up the river water—had become mere prerequisites to a larger project.

Long afterwards, many of those who had created Expo would admit that if they had had any idea of what the effort would require, they might not have taken it on. But by the time that dawned, it was too late to back out gracefully. The only exit was straight ahead through forty months that would change the city as much as it had changed in forty years.

The thing that pulled it through was a singularity of purpose and cohesion few cities could muster. World's fairs, which involve lots of money, lots of people and drastic changes in the city's life, are typically riven with disputes. In Spokane the odds were long enough and the stakes large enough that the city went on a kind of emergency footing. Differences were laid aside. The deadline ruled out equivocation and delay. Every resource and every person in the city was subject to being drafted to the cause.

The Expo board of directors included forty-eight opinion leaders from all phases of life in the community. The executive committee that would take care of the day-to-day decisions was made up of twelve people who represented most of the city's financial resources: Roderick Lindsay of Lincoln First Federal Savings and Loan Association; James P. Brennan of First National Bank; James G. Critzer of Critzer Equipment Company; James P. Cowles of Cowles Publishing Company; Vern W. Johnson of Vern W. Johnson and Sons, Inc., general contractors; E.A. Coon of Seattle-First National Bank; Kinsey M. Robinson of Washington Water Power Company; Philip H. Stanton of Washington Trust Bank; Edwin J. McWilliams of Fidelity Mutual Savings Bank; Bruce H. McPhaden of Kaiser Aluminum Company; Lawrence V. Brown of Pack River Company; and Joseph J. Rosenfield of SRO Favorite Theaters, Inc. Significantly, nearly all those on the executive committee were the chief executives in their own banks and companies. When money was needed, these people wouldn't have to go back and make a presentation to a budget committee. The committee was headed up by Roderick A. Lindsay, a powerful personality who had taken over his father's bank in the depths of the Depression and built it into the multi-million-dollar Lincoln Savings and Loan Association.

But even Lindsay and his band of chief executive officers did not have the wherewithal to put on a world's fair by themselves. The plan was that the city, with its access to tax revenues and government aid, would acquire ownership of the land along the river and build a park on it. This park, however, would be loaned as the site of a six-month exposition— which would leave in its wake a civic center and all sorts of other residuals the city could afford no other way.

The plan almost floundered from the start because a city bond issue, which was to provide $5.7 million to create a park on the river, failed to get the necessary 60 percent approval (though it did

get a healthy majority, 56 percent). The only option left to the city to raise the money was the dreaded business and occupations tax, the very one that had caused a revolt against city government a decade earlier. Mayor David H. Rodgers (who succeeded Neil Fosseen in 1967) called a mass meeting of the city's organizations, ranging from the Chamber of Commerce to the League of Women Voters and National Association for the Advancement of Colored People. He asked for and received a concensus that the council should raise the money by imposing a new business and occupations tax. On the night the city council voted to impose the new tax, only one person stood up to protest. Spokane had begun to unite behind a purpose.

One reason such a small city could put on a fair of this size was that the whole of city government became virtually a part of the Expo staff. Mayor Rodgers had a solid four votes on the council to approve anything necessary to make Expo work. Sometimes, to keep up with relentless Expo deadlines, city staff members took actions on the career-risking trust that the council would back them up retroactively.

City Manager F. Sylvin Fulwiler had assigned the city's chief engineer, Glen A. Yake, to head up city government's part of the effort. Robust, popular, often controversial, Yake had shepherded hundreds of engineering projects from design to approval in his thirty years with the city, and no one was in a better position to coordinate all the machinery of local government and dozens of private contractors.

Yake's first job was to secure for the city ownership of the riverfront property. There were thirty owners of land to be dealt with one by one, but the important three were the railroads. The Union Pacific alone had once estimated that its properties on the riverfront were worth

about $16 million. The Expo board and the city replied at an early meeting that they would like to see the railroads simply donate the land. This idea was the cause of open merriment among railroad officials at one of the initial meetings. But Yake and King Cole kept after the railroads with an argument that finally proved persuasive (and, as it turned out, true). The railroads, they argued, could donate the primary land, but hold on to fringe property. The new park would increase the value of these surrounding parcels of land so much the railroads would profit in the long run.

The railroads finally capitulated, donating all of the riverfront property. But they said they would sign only when the city had straightened out legal complications. What seemed like a reasonable

stipulation in fact became one of the major obstacles to producing Expo. In nearly a century of operations through Spokane, the three railroads had built up a tangled mass of trades, agreements, and legal technicalities which encumbered every piece of property. Yake and the city's legal staff had to straighten out these encumbrances to get clear title, and couldn't do so without railroad cooperation. But railroad officials, sitting in their offices in Chicago or Milwaukee, far from the pressing deadlines of Spokane's exposition, appeared to give the situation a low priority. When Yake would try to contact them with an urgent problem, sometimes his call was returned and sometimes it wasn't.

When it wasn't, he called Jim Cowles, the younger grandson of the founder of

As soon as the riverfront railroad tracks were dismantled, the wrecking ball went to work on the Great Northern depot. On February 5, 1973, the clock tower warned that only 450 days remained until the World's Fair would begin. The tower itself was left in the park as a reminder of the role railroads played in Spokane's development. (EWSHS)

Spokane's newspapers. James and his brother, William Cowles, III, had taken over the family business in the late 1960s, including management of two and one-half blocks of very valuable downtown property. Though they were wont to caution others against putting a Cowles out front in the Expo effort—it might stir up the old questions about the family running Spokane—the two brothers played a key role in the fifteen-year effort to upgrade the city's center.

James Cowles is invariably listed as one of the people most important to making Expo a success. He got involved in many aspects of the fair, but his specific assignment from the Expo board of directors was to deal with the railroads. His influence with them was not entirely clear to anyone. Apparently the Cowles Publishing Company took its considerable banking business to a bank with

strong ties to the Union Pacific. Also, the Cowles-owned Inland Paper Company was a major shipper with railroads. But Cowles' effectiveness with the sluggish railroad bureaucracies appeared to be based upon dogged persistence as much as anything. At one point he had architect Tom Adkison work through a weekend, redrawing the Expo plans to show a world's fair taking place on a site still containing remnants of the railroads. Cowles took the plans to Milwaukee to show railroad officials *they* were going to be the ones embarrassed if things didn't start to happen on the site. When John Kenefick, the president of Union Pacific Railroad, came to Spokane for a pre-Expo function, he leaned over to Mayor Rodgers and said, "Would you mind pointing out this fellow Jim Cowles to me?" "I got the impression," Rodgers said later, "that he had had some pretty

City manager F. Sylvin Fulwiler (left) and chief engineer Glen A. Yake hammer out details of city's acquisition of riverfront land.

firm conversations with Jim."

A remarkable thing about Spokane's Expo effort is that it had many obstacles, but each time there seemed to be someone especially equipped to lift it over the hurdles. If the railroads were going to give up their stations on the riverfront, they would have to agree to share facilities in the Northern Pacific station at the south edge of the city's business district. Approval of such consolidations by the U.S. Interstate Commerce Commission often took months. In Spokane's case it took seven days. The reason was that the chairman of the U.S. Senate committee that oversees ICC business was Senator Warren G. Magnuson of Washington State. Senator Magnuson, one of the Senate's most powerful legislators, arranged for a long list of federal subsidies to Expo, only one example of which was the $11.5 million Federal Pavilion "tent."

The Expo plan drawn up by Economic Research Associates had as one of its essential requirements the construction of a $7.5 million convention hall and auditorium. This was both necessary for the Exposition and was one of the main prizes the city expected to get for all this effort. This, people in Spokane thought, would be the ideal contribution of the State of Washington.

Getting the state to go along, however, was going to be difficult because the legislature was both controlled by interests on the west side of the state and in a conservative mood.

To deal with the legislature the Expo board called in Luke Williams, Jr. Luke and his brother Chuck had invented in their garage in the Spokane Valley what was to become a part of the American scene: the lighted-up sign panel capable of flashing ever-changing messages and pictures. Their Spokane-based company, American Sign & Indicator, built signs for customers around the world, from New York City's Times Square to Saudi

Arabia, and in the process Luke had become both wealthy and well-known in business circles. And, he was active in Chamber of Commerce and conservative Republican circles. Expo chairman Roderick Lindsay, a former Democratic state legislator himself, could deal with Democrats in the legislature. It was the Republicans who might be a problem, so Williams, reminded of his civic duties and apprised of the situation, was sent off in his private airplane to talk to business and Republican friends around the state. The legislature provided the $7.5 million original appropriation and later supplemented that with another three million dollars.

When even that second appropriation ran short—for the plans for the Opera House became more ambitious as time went on—Williams recruited Vicki McNeill, an experienced local fundraiser for charities, to contact donors all over the city and state to raise another one million dollars for finishing touches.

This is how Expo would be built: with volunteer work and mostly outside money. The cost of preparing the fair site alone would be a minimum of sixty million dollars, and that kind of money did not exist in Spokane. Spokane businesses had pooled six million dollars in "seed" money to get the effort organized, and besides had taxed themselves to spruce up the downtown area with trees, new benches, and new street lamps. The rest of the money was picked up bit by bit. When there was no money to buy out a thriving motel occupying part of the prospective fair site, Mayor Rodgers called the Comstock Foundation, a local philanthropic group. It bought the land and gave it to the city. When there had to be a new bridge passing through the site at Washington Street, City Councilman Del Jones and Glen Yake persuaded the state's Urban Arterial Board to declare the situation an emergency and put up the funds. When money for putting finishing touches on the site ran low, City Councilman Jack O'Brien suggested the ultimately successful stratagem of applying for a grant from the U.S. Economic Development Agency on the grounds that a successful Expo would boost Spokane's economy.

If preparing a site for the fair was a scramble, bringing exhibitors to it was even more so. Lee Iaccoca, then president of the Ford Motor Company, said his first response when it was suggested that Ford become an exhibitor in Spokane was, "Where the hell's Spokane?" That was the essence of the problem for Expo recruiters. Many doubted five million people would go so far out of the way to visit the fair, and so potential exhibitors were tempted to say no without even looking the proposition over. King Cole's strategy was to have Spokanites with national contacts get a representative to at least come out and take a look. Once here, the national representative was entertained in private homes, chauffered around, introduced to friendly contractors and union leaders who guaranteed there would be no labor disputes to contend with. Spokane, it seemed, could arrange just about anything for an exhibitor. In the fall of 1972, Walt Toly, the recently retired president of Columbia Heating and Light and now head of the effort to entice American exhibitors to Expo, brought top executives from General Motors, Ford, Kodak, IBM, and other companies to Spokane for a sales pitch. He tramped them across the site and then took them to the YMCA building on Havermale Island and showed them slides of what the fair would look like. There was just one problem. The feature attraction, the river, was almost bone dry. Toly explained that during most of the Fair this rock canyon would be boiling with snowmelt. Then he said, "Look, I'll show you." Several miles up

the river Kinsey Robinson, president of the Washington Water Power Company, had personally ordered the dams opened, and at noon, as scheduled, a wall of water smashed through the basalt canyon even as the executives watched. They were impressed.

Expo's breakthrough with international exhibitors came in the wake of a breakthrough in international politics. The very day President Richard Nixon was in Moscow signing agreements which were part of the general warming of U.S.—USSR relations known as "detente," King Cole was sitting in the George V Hotel bar with Boris Borisov, chairman of the Soviet Chamber of Commerce and Industry. In the spirit of detente the Soviets committed to an immense exhibit that would cover a full acre and was four times as large as the Soviet exhibit at the 1962 Seattle World's Fair. This early, large-scale participation by the Soviet Union did more than anything else to legitimize Expo '74 as an international exhibit.

The first foreign exhibitor to sign on was, naturally enough, Canada. It agreed to occupy the key island which now bears its name. But that agreement precipitated a major crisis in Expo's development. One year before the opening of Expo the national Canadian government in Ottawa decided almost routinely to reduce a budget deficit by eliminating the funds which had been set aside for the Spokane exhibit. News of this caused near panic in Spokane. Other exhibitors then being courted—indeed, perhaps the others that had already committed—might wonder if this really was a "world's fair" if even this close neighbor would not participate.

Luckily, Western Canadians reacted swiftly and angrily to their national government's decision. Editorials in Canadian newspapers blasted the decision while bumper stickers appeared on Canadian cars that read, "To Hell With Ottawa,

We're Going To Spokane." The protests caused the national Canadian government to reverse its decision. It is entirely possible that long-time friends to the north saved Spokane's world's fair.

The very audacity of the whole Expo project had guaranteed there would be constant crises like this, which piled pressure on top of heavy work loads. Everyone knew, Expo Executive Vice President David Peterson would say later, that they were either involved in one of the great experiments of urban revitalization, or an ignominious flop that would be recounted by the press all over the world: "People said, 'You can't do it, you can't do it.' Then we had the state involved, then the federal government. Then we were in *Time* magazine and everybody in the nation was watching us. You feel that tension when you go home at night. If we didn't make it, Spokane was going to be 'The Little City That Couldn't.'"

The U.S. Department of Commerce was among those getting nervous. It had both money and prestige invested in the Spokane Fair, and it didn't want to see a flop. It was accustomed to watching world's fairs develop, furthermore, and no doubt it had never seen a fair built like this—by people who went about begging every board as it was needed.

Early in the summer before Expo, Department of Commerce officials called Rod Lindsay to Washington, D.C., and flatly threatened to ask Congress to withdraw its support for the fair if changes were not made in its management. Whether department officials would or could make good on such a threat was another question. But any open debate about the fair at this point, when the city was beginning its publicity campaign to get visitors to come, would have been disastrous. Besides, Lindsay and other members of the executive board did not necessarily disagree that a shake-up would be healthy. Lindsay decided on his

own to take the department's advice. He interviewed three professional fair managers and hired Petr Spurney as general manager.

Many of the executive board were livid when Lindsay returned to Spokane and told them what he had done. There was a fierce proprietary feeling about Expo by this time, and board members resented the federal agency's meddling. The "sense of command" so many admired in Lindsay now began to look like sheer arbitrariness. Around the board table there were loud voices, flushed faces, angry tapping of pencils. For the first time the unity which had brought the city this far was threatened. But Lindsay reminded them that there was no turning back at this point, and the crisis passed.

Many of those who had worked on Expo for three years before Petr Spurney arrived felt Spurney gave the impression that he had personally made it a success, and they resented it. But most would concede that Spurney contributed to the fair by providing specialized knowledge of concessionaires, organizing advertising

Expo president King F. Cole (left) and J. Welles Henderson, U.S. commissioner general for Expo '74, survey construction at the Expo site.

and publicity, and scheduling on-site entertainment.

Spokane's distinction in the history of world's fairs is that it was the first to so thoroughly subordinate the short-term celebration to the long-term benefits. Such facilities as the Opera House, housing for the Carousel (which served as a "Bavarian Beer Garden" for the duration of the fair) and Boeing Amphitheater were all planned not for a fair but for the future.

The fair's general architect, Tom Adkison, was a long-time member of the Spokane Park Board. Always, as he laid out the park for Expo, he kept in mind the park that would follow it. He conceptualized a park of contrasts. Isolated pathways would open suddenly onto broad fields. The sense of an untamed, unmanageable river in the north channels would be heightened by suspended bridges which swung over the water, as if it were too wild to touch. The south channel Forebay, by contrast, would be highly structured and sculpturesque, with steps descending right into the water and bridges with legs firmly sunk in the slow-moving water.

City and country would mix in the park. Hollows and hills suggest rural beauty, while the Great Northern Clock Tower, the Carousel, and the Parsian beauty of the Washington Street Bridge would represent the best in urban forms. The new was blended with the old when lamp poles which had stood on Spokane downtown streets since the 1920s were shortened, fitted with new glass and used to light the park's pathways.

These plans were translated into a fair by dozens of contractors under the direction of general contractor Vern Johnson of Spokane. Until late in the spring of 1974 the view through the chain link fences that surrounded the site was one of mud, materials, and machinery in motion. Because much of the grass was

saved to be laid down at the last minute, people who looked at the site from the outside wondered if it could possibly be shaped up by opening day. In fact it was finished a day early.

It was very cool the morning of May 4, 1974, 38 degrees at 6:00 a.m. But as the sun rose in a clear blue sky the air warmed and took on the sweet vibrancy typical of Spokane mornings in early spring or late fall. Twenty thousand people crowded around the north side of the new Opera House to observe opening day ceremonies. Expo officials, representatives of the nine foreign nations exhibiting at the fair, and local political representatives, gathered on a stage floating in the Forebay. President Nixon (who had just a few days earlier released the "Watergate tapes" which would lead to his resignation only four months later) arrived shortly before noon to declare Expo '74 "open to the world."

Eighty-five thousand went through the gates on opening day. The millionth visitor showed up June 8, and by the time the six-month fair was over, 5.6 million had purchased tickets, pushing attendance over projections by a million.

Fair-goers could visit nine national exhibits (from Australia, Canada, the Federal Republic of Germany, Iran, Japan, the Republic of China, the Republic of Korea, the Phillipines, the Soviet Union, and the United States; seven exhibits by Northwest states and Canadian provinces; sixty-two industrial exhibits (including General Motors, Ford Motor Company, Kodak, and Kaiser Aluminum); and twenty-six "special category" exhibits (ranging from the Afro-American exhibit to that of the Washington State Wheat Commission). Four open-air stages, including one floating in the Forebay behind the Opera House, were booked through the day and evening with entertainment from all over the world. A central food fair and a dozen specialty restaurants, brass bands, mimes, jugglers, and magicians, plus a daily average of 30,000 people swarming the pathways, added up to an experience hard to imagine now on the peaceful grounds of Riverfront Park.

One of the two most popular exhibits was the Soviet Pavilion, where an unsmiling bronze Vladimir Lenin welcomed visitors into an acre of dioramas, scientific displays, and a lime-colored fantasy representing the biosphere. The other crowd-pleaser was under the tent of the U.S. Pavilion, where giant insects dangling overhead carefully arranging heaps of junk mocked the human propensity toward spoiling their own nest. In the IMAX Theater an audience listening to an Indian the size of a four-story building talk about the environment suddenly found their chairs seemingly falling out from under them as they "flew" through the narrows of the Grand Canyon, skimming above the river. The Korean exhibit featured "The Sounds of Nature"—recorded sounds of birds, voices, and moving water—while the Iranian exhibit displayed ancient Persian artifacts. Japan constructed a Japanese Garden at the entrance to a theater where costumed women performed traditional dances. From the belting cheeriness of the "Up With People" singers in the General Motors Pavilion one could descend into the cave-like darkness of a section of the Australian Pavilion and look a rare reptile or an inverted bat in the eye. An art exhibit in the new Convention Center displayed the works of Audubon, Remington, Russell, Wyeth, Grandma Moses, Mark Tobey, and other American masters; a short walk beyond that was the gaudy Midway. And at every turn there was the rediscovered river itself. A record runoff that May and June sent a canyon full of water tumbling over itself and foaming white in its rush to the Falls.

What a strange sight it was for a Spokanite of that era, strolling along the river on a fragrant summer evening, to look across the reflecting waters of the Forebay to a renewed cityscape and see the Opera House lit up with a famous name on the marquee—Jack Benny; John Denver; Bob Hope; Van Cliburn; Victor Borge; Jose Feliciano; the Philadelphia or Los Angeles Philharmonics; the Joffrey Ballet; the Leningrad Ballet.

During the six months of the fair, a series of symposia held in nearby buildings explored the large questions that a world

Spokane's past was showcased at Expo's Folklife Festival. Visitors could enjoy the daily logging exhibitions and the authentic Indian dances or watch their names stitched into a huge quilt. In one of the most popular exhibits fairgoers could pan gold brought in from an Idaho claim. (EWSHS)

Facing page: *The Spokane Falls at full flood in springtime. James Glover first viewed the falls in Spokane in May 1873. Today one can imagine the effect the thundering and gurgling water had on Glover during his two hour vigil by the falls when he first arrived in an unsettled Spokane. Photo by Richard Heinzen*

Pages 98-99: *Duncan Gardens in Manito Park. Photos by Richard Heinzen*

exposition on the environment had raised. Authorities from around the world came to Spokane to discuss the pollution of the oceans, air, soil and the exhaustion of natural resources—dangers which, strange as it would seem later, had hardly begun to penetrate world consciousness.

Expo itself was a practical statement on such problems. It was publicized across the country and was studied by many other cities as a model of what a community could do if it perceived a problem, found a plan, and worked together. Almost unnoticed in the excitement of the fair was the fact that Spokane had built (mostly with federal funds) a sewage treatment plant which cost more than the Federal Pavilion, the Opera House, and all the landscaping of Riverfront Park combined. This project, which was under way before Expo, had been supplemented by a massive, Expo-inspired study of the entire Spokane River basin. The study helped cease the flushing of pollutants into the Spokane River by mines, lumber mills, plants, and towns between Idaho and the Columbia River. Within a few years these efforts brought the river closer to its natural purity than it had been in this century.

Expo had begun to have its intended effect on the downtown long before opening day. The JC Penney Company, impressed by Spokane's revival, reversed a company policy of rebuilding only in shopping centers and established a new store in Spokane's downtown. Its old building was remodeled and occupied by Nordstrom. The skywalk system, a remnant of the Ebasco Plan, began in the early seventies to link all buildings downtown, creating a second downtown one story above the first, a unique idea that gained national publicity. A new hotel on the riverfront (the Sheraton), two new bank towers (Sea-First and Washington Trust), the new Cowles-built parking ga-

rage, and such notable restorations as the 1889 Building and the Bennett Block added to what would be one of the most successful examples of urban revival in the country.

At the center of this revival, as planned, was the new Riverfront Park. When it opened in 1976 people swarmed to it—settling all doubts about whether a city-center park could attract people.

The single most popular aspect of the new park turned out to be the seventy-year-old Carousel from Natatorium Park. Purchased years earlier through a city-wide fund drive, it immediately began contributing $50,000 per year to the park's upkeep.

The Carousel is a symbol of continuity in Spokane. Children who ride the Carousel today could be the great-great-grandchildren of those who rode it when it came to Spokane in 1911.

The Carousel stands at the corner of Howard and Spokane Falls Boulevard—right back where this story began. Jimmy Glover himself ordained the location and dimensions of this, Spokane's first, intersection. Fifty feet to the east, a grassy spot just above the Forebay now, is where James Nosler, the hardworking but tragic pioneer had his first land office in Spokane Falls. Diagonally across the boulevard is the corner where the irrepressible Anthony Cannon had his store and bank. Directly across the street is the Coeur d'Alene Hotel, Dutch Jake's building, the very heap of bricks which once vibrated with piano music and the desperate laughter of the miners and maidens of Spokane's turn-of-the-century honkey-tonk district.

What stories this little spot of earth has seen.

And will see yet. For we come to the end of a book only. Tomorrow morning the streets of Spokane will be lit by the first low beams of sunlight, and the story goes on.

Above: *Cannon Hill Park, near the crest of the south hill, is one of sixty parks in the city. Courtesy, Richard Heinzen*

Right: *The Spokane-Nishinomiya Japanese Tea Garden, in Manito Park, is considered one of the most authentic in the U.S. Courtesy, Richard Heinzen*

Facing page: *This 1981 view of an old barn in the wheatfields of the Spokane Valley looks as though it could have been taken a century ago. Courtesy, Earl Roberge*

Right: *The first snow delicately transforms the Spokane landscape. Courtesy, Richard Heinzen*

Right: *These unusual rock formations, known familiarly as the "Bowl and Pitcher," have attracted thousands of visitors to Riverside State Park, three miles northwest of the city. The rocks are remnants of a one-mile-thick basaltic shelf that once blanketed the Inland Empire. Land for Riverside State Park was secured by Aubrey L. White, the founding president of the Spokane Park Board. The suspension bridge near the "Bowl and Pitcher" was built by the Civilian Conservation Corps, and opened in May of 1941. Courtesy, Richard MacLeod*

102

Above: *Only thirty miles northeast of the city, Mt. Spokane attracts skiers, snowmobilers, and other Inland Empire winter sports enthusiasts. Mt. Spokane State Park is one of four major ski resorts within ninety minutes of Spokane. Courtesy, Richard Heinzen*

*In the Palouse, a crop
duster sprays a field
of mustard plants.
During the growing
season, crop dusters
dance like bees over
the rolling fields of
the Palouse. Photo
by Colin Mulvany.
Courtesy, The* Spokes-
man Review

Left: *Spokane pioneer James Monaghan had this home built for his wife, who died shortly before its completion in 1895. The Monaghan home, at East 217 Boone Avenue, has been used as a music conservatory by Gonzaga University since 1939. Courtesy, Richard Heinzen (EWSHS)*

Left: *The dramatic Spokane Opera House graces Riverfront Park in this 1985 view. Courtesy, Richard Heinzen*

Left: *Downtown Spo-
kane had regained its
vitality in this 1980
view of the Parkade
Plaza. Courtesy, Earl
Roberge*

Left: *This 1976 aerial shows the expanse of Spokane from the falls to the mountains. Courtesy, Earl Roberge*

Left: *The renovated interior of one of the first movie theaters in Spokane. It opened in 1915 and was called The Clemmer. It was also used for live entertainment, including performances by a young Bing Crosby. It later became the State Theater. In 1988 it was restored and renamed The Met by Paul Sandifur Jr. and is used as a center for the performing arts. Photo by Barros and Barros*

An aerial view (looking north) of Gonzaga University, showing, in the foreground, the Ralph E. and Helen Higgins Foley Center. The library opened in 1992. Behind it is the original Gonzaga Administration building built in 1887, one of the largest buildings in the region at the time. St. Aloysius Church is located next to it. The university and the neighborhood were built by pioneering Jesuit missionaries. Early in the century the neighborhood was sometimes referred to as "The Little Vatican" because within its one mile-by-half mile radius it contained the university, two high schools, two grade schools, an orphanage and a retirement home, all Catholic. Courtesy of Libby Photographers and Gonzaga University

Left: *Crowds of Spo-kanites meet and relax at Riverfront Park, where the Great Northern Railroad once had its railyard. Courtesy, Richard Heinzen*

Below: *Centennial Sculpture 1881-1981 in the Forebay of Riverfront Park commemorates the passage of 100 years since Spokane was officially* incorporated. It was created by Harold Balazs, Spokane's best known sculptor. Photo by Richard Heinzen*

Left: *As they did for centuries before white settlers arrived, Native Americans gathered on the banks of the Spokane River in 1995 for traditional dances and games. The Northwest Indian Encampment and Pow Wow in River-front Park became an annual event follow-ing its inception in 1989. Courtesy, The* Spokesman Review

Above: *The gently rolling hills of the Palouse country sweep to the horizon in this 1983 view. Courtesy, Earl Roberge*

Right: *The historic Spokane Flour Mill has a new life as a multi-level shopping mall. The Flour Mill began to tie the north side of the river to the life of downtown. Courtesy, Richard Heinzen*

Left: *The clock tower and U.S. Pavilion frame this view of Riverfront Park on a sunny September afternoon in 1976. Courtesy, Richard Heinzen*

Below: *Spokanites take time to enjoy a romantic stroll in the park. Courtesy, Richard Heinzen*

A serene nighttime view of the Spokane River reflecting light from the Spokane Opera House and the Great Northern Railroad Tower. Photo by Richard Heinzen

Facing page: *The gon-
dola ride across the
Spokane River contin-
ues to give Spokanites
and visitors a thrilling
view of the falls. Cour-
tesy, Richard Heinzen*

*This May 1974 over-
view of Expo shows it
in full swing.*

Above: *Dancers from China prepare to perform at Expo '74.*

Right: *A bust of Lenin greeted visitors to the USSR pavilion, the largest foreign exhibit at Expo.*

Far left: *The Spokane River forebay lights up at night as Expo visitors get a dramatic view of the sprawling fairgrounds.*

Left: *Jeanne Lewis, a nine-year-old from Toppenish, Washington, gets ready for a dance contest.*

Below: *USSR National Day featured a performance by the Moiseyev Dance Company.*

VIII

SPOKANE DIVIDED

In his study of Expo, *The Fair and the Falls*, historian William T. Youngs asked how Spokane was able to pull off such a feat, and came to the answers that have long since become part of the city's lore. Spokane may have been small, but it had a cadre of business leaders who controlled their own companies and could act on their own convictions. "The men who gathered at meetings of Spokane Unlimited were able to raise a million dollars without leaving the room," Youngs wrote. Also, Expo was a great enough task that others in the community were confronted with a clear choice to support it or sink it; there was no room for quibbling. King Cole, the mastermind of Expo, remarked that one thing he admired when he arrived in Spokane was that, "they had so little of what we commonly think of when we say the word 'politics.'" Finally, the business community and Spokane city government were in perfect step. Since each had its strengths and each had its limitations, Cole said, "we traded off and got things done."

Twenty-five years later Spokane presented a very different picture. At the end of the 20th century, every step city leadership took was marked by rancorous debates, divisive election campaigns, and lawsuits that from time to time went all the way to the state

An aerial view of Spokane in 1998, looking southwest. Photo by Libby Air Photo

Supreme Court. The mayor of Spokane and the Chamber of Commerce were not speaking to each other. The City Council could hardly make an important decision without the fear that it would be overturned in a plebiscite. In 1998, Washington State University political scientist Nicolas Lovrich presented polling data to a Chamber of Commerce group that showed Spokane had a larger segment of cynical citizens than most cities, including larger cities such as Seattle, Minneapolis and San Francisco.

What happened to the spirit that created Expo? The simple answer is that it remained what it always had been—but the times had changed. Leaders acting decisively on their own initiative did not take time to build consensuses, making challenges to their decisions inevitable in the long run. The ethic of "no politics" was so handy to those trying to get things done that they forgot that dissent had its role, too. The cooperation between city government and business that seemed so natural in the 1960s came to be seen, after the Vietnam and Watergate decades, as collusion. In other words, what changed was not so much Spokane as the way business would have to be done.

In the 1950s, city government supervised only the most basic services, parks, policing, patching roads, and the like. Five commissioners supervised these functions, each responsible for a particular area of government. They were responsive to citizens because their

Spokane's annual Bloomsday Race attracts the best athletes from all over the world. It is also a popular social event for citizens who walk or run the course. Started in 1977 by Don Kardong, an Olympic marathoner, the race draws about 50,000 participants each year. Photo by Sandra Bancroft-Billings. Courtesy, The Spokesman-Review

Neal Fosseen, the first mayor of Spokane under the city manager system initiated in 1960. Fosseen was elected twice and served until 1967. Photo by Eric Galey. Courtesy, Eastern Washington University

duties were listed right after their names and they clearly had the ability to hire and fire to carry out those duties. If the sewers weren't built or if a corrupt policeman was revealed, there was no question which commissioner voters could hold responsible at the next election.

But with each commissioner intent on showing a good record in his own area, none had reason to see the larger picture. They dragged their feet, for example, in cleaning up a river polluted by sewage. Solving such a major problem would have required sustained cooperation and sacrifice in other areas of city government, both of which went against the grain of the commissioner system.

Spokane's business leaders, forced to acknowledge the drastic changes coming over American urban life due to the automobile, were the first to realize Spokane's form of government was a roadblock to more ambitious goals. Spokane's most influential business leaders proposed the city manager system—a favorite with business leaders because it resembled corporate governance. The selling point was that a professional manager would replace the amiable, but not particularly competent, politicians. The opponents' argument against the city manager system—that "the proposed form, in the interest of claimed efficiency, sacrifices democracy"—was not particularly effective, because democracy appeared to have little to do with patching the streets and the other modest tasks of local government. In March 1960, voters adopted the new form of government.

Having championed the city manager system, business leaders wanted to make sure it worked. In a smoke-filled room they reviewed possible candidates for city council and selected a sterling group that ran almost as a party ticket under the rubric "The Citizen Seven." The business leaders persuaded Neal Fosseen, a vice president of Old National Bank, Spokane's most prestigious financial institution, to run for mayor. It was a brilliant move. Four decades later, the harshest critics of city manager government would say, "But, Fosseen, now *there* was a mayor!"

Fosseen knew Spokane and its citizens. He had helped build Spokane, literally brick-by-brick. He spent his summers working for his father's

company, Washington Brick and Lime Company, which supplied the bricks for the majority of Spokane's old brick buildings. Fosseen saw the foundations of Spokane laid in another sense as well. An Eagle Scout himself, he was deeply involved in the city-wide scouting movement, thus getting to know many of the city's future leaders while they were still teenagers.

By the 1930s, when he had taken over direction of the family's brick business, Fosseen was already someone people turned to for help with their problems. A friend who was head of the area's U.S. Marine Reserve unit complained to Fosseen that the Marines had no budget for an adequate drill hall. Fosseen surveyed business friends and found the Marines a large room in what was later the Bon Marché Building. The friend decided Fosseen could be useful and talked him into taking a commission in the Marine Reserve.

When World War II broke out, Fosseen was sent to the South Pacific, an

Medical service has been one of Spokane's key industries through-out the 20th century. Beginning in the 1950s, Spokane physicians and researchers began coronary research which received national and international attention. The research continues at the Heart Institute (foreground), which opened in 1991. In the background is the Sacred Heart Medical Center. Courtesy, Sacred Heart Medical Center

Luke Williams, businessman, often involved in local, as well as national politics. Courtesy, The Spokesman-Review

The Spokane Club on the corner of Riverside and Monroe was the informal gathering place of Spokane's business and governing elite after it opened in 1910. The Georgian Revival-style building was designed by architects Kirtland Cutter and Karl Malmgren. The statue in the foreground memorializes Ensign James Robert Monaghan, who was killed in action during the Spanish-American War, in 1899. Monaghan, a member of one of Spokane's founding families, was the first graduate of the U.S. Naval Academy from Washington state. Courtesy, Northwest Room, Spokane Public Library

officer in the Marine's supply apparatus. From Guadalcanal Fosseen wrote back to his old friend on Spokane's Athletic Round Table, Joe Albi, that a big problem among the troops was boredom while they waited for the generals to decide which island to attack next. Some time later Major Fosseen got a message that the Navy had just delivered to the Guadalcanal docks some strange looking cargo. Fosseen claimed it. The custom-made wooden boxes, shipped as official cargo through the U.S. Naval Depot in Spokane, contained slot machines from the Athletic Round Table's club room, reconfigured for the Marines so that the "lemon loser" icons were embellished with unflattering cartoons of the wartime prime minister of Japan.

Much later Fosseen would tell this story only as an amusing anecdote. In fact it is an insight into Spokane's political workings in that era. At mid-century Spokane was a relatively small, homogeneous place. When Joe Albi—the tireless worker for Spokane's amateur sports for whom the city's stadium

would one day be named—occasionally needed the assistance of city government, he did not deal with a faceless bureaucracy. Mayor Fosseen, in turn, had no trouble communicating with Albi—or with former boy scouts or Marine veterans, or with a long list of charitable and educational institutions with which he was affiliated.

As business's choice for mayor, Fosseen could call upon the help of other business leaders. Sharp-minded owners of local businesses were available to the city with a phone call. Every major business in town expected its brightest young executives to devote some of their evenings to thinking about the problems of city government. Lawyers, architects, accountants and other professionals who would send anyone else fat bills for advice, sat on city boards and committees at no charge.

Businessman Luke Williams recalled the evening he was drafted to city service. He went to the regular Thursday night dinner at the Spokane Club—that oak, brass and crystal headquarters of

Spokane leadership. When Williams looked around for a place to sit he saw a chair open next to just-elected Mayor Fosseen. Williams sat down and proceeded to tell the mayor all the things the city was doing wrong. Fosseen replied, "Well, Luke, you seem to know so much about the problems, why don't you run for city council and help us solve them?" At that time, Williams was launching a new business, the American Sign and Indicator Company, and was also involved in national politics. But he felt his bluff had been called. Williams ran and was elected to the city council.

Ten years later it was Williams, the self-described "far-right conservative," who was representing the city in the state capitol when it came time to ask the governor to donate a $10 million Opera House to Spokane, a classic example of the very pork-barrel political exchanges conservatives opposed. Williams later admitted he found the role awkward. But, he had long-since signed on to the larger effort. His personal politics and his loyalty to Spokane clashed, and loyalty won.

No one could accuse Williams of taking politics lightly. He devoted much of his life to it; he was described in Theodore White's *The Making of the President, 1964*, as one of those who had gained the Republican nomination for Barry Goldwater. But, speaking pointedly amidst Spokane's divisive political scene two decades later, Williams said he felt Spokane was so small one had to search for points of agreement rather than differences, including political differences. He offered another surprising instance from his own experience. Though he had often campaigned against them, Washington's powerful Democratic senators Warren Magnuson and Henry Jackson did anything they could to protect American Sign and Indicator and the 600 Spokane constitu-

The Honorable Tom Foley, Speaker of the U. S. House of Representatives from 1989 to 1994. He represented Spokane and the surrounding Fifth Congressional District from 1964 to 1994. Photo by Sandra Bancroft-Billings. Courtesy, The Spokesman-Review

ents of theirs it employed. In fact, Williams, one of the country's better known Republican operatives, and Jackson, one of the country's most powerful Democrats, became close friends. Jackson's help proved indispensable to the growth of Williams' company around the world. Once, when Williams was thanking Jackson yet again for his help on some business matter, Jackson said, "Luke, I'll ask one favor in return. Get off Tom Foley's back." As a 'sort of a hobby,' Williams had given special support to campaigns every two years trying to unseat Spokane's Democratic Congressman, Tom Foley. It was well known that Jackson had brought Foley into politics and acted as a mentor to the future Speaker of the House of Representatives. Jackson had high hopes for Foley's future in the House, if he could survive the politics of Spokane. Williams figured he owed Jackson. He agreed, and from

The Mount St. Helen's volcano in May 1980 spewed ash over Spokane and the surrounding area. Removing the ash became a major difficulty. Years later ash could still be seen along the roadsides in Eastern Washington. Courtesy, The Spokesman-Review

David Rodgers, mayor from 1967 to 1977. A businessman himself, Rodgers coordinated city government's contribution to the Expo era. Courtesy, David Rodgers

that point on he never again contributed to an anti-Foley campaign, even after Jackson's death in 1983.

Beneath the level of party affiliations, elective titles, and economic interests, Spokane's pre-Expo politics were a thicket of personal relationships resulting from lifetimes spent on the affairs of one small geographical area. This "Old Boys' Club," as it came to be called, believed that things got done when people with resources cooperated.

As business leaders saw it, city government was a natural extension of the cooperative enterprise. For the first 17 years of city manager government—first under Fosseen and then David Rodgers, the focused and efficient political leader through Expo—it operated just that way.

In the first post-Expo mayoral election of 1977, business preferred a banking executive, Tom Garrett, for mayor. But the establishment was surprised by the entry into the race by television news broadcaster Ron Bair, whose familiarity with voters, after two decades of reading news to them on KXLY TV, made him a landslide winner. What the role of a television broadcaster in city hall might be, stumped the business community. Luckily, in those ebb tide years of Expo there were few big decisions pending.

Bair made one welcome contribution to city council meetings. He had a suave humor that seemed to calm council meetings that had become raucous when citizens literally lined up to upbraid the council for failures of every sort.

During his third year in office, Bair's skills as a broadcaster came into unexpected demand when Mount St. Helens in the southwestern part of the state erupted. Half a mountain exploded into the air. The finest dust rose into the atmosphere and slowly settled across Washington, Idaho and Montana. In Spokane, the dust, a grayish-white grit so fine that the push of a broom would send it swirling into the air, covered everything with a blanket of ash up to an inch thick. When Mayor Bair appeared on television to report that scientists at Washington State University determined it was okay to work with the dust, people strapped paper masks over their mouths and noses and began sweeping and shoveling it off walks and roofs. Gradually the white ash disappeared under ordinary dust and Mount St. Helens' dust formed just another layer of Spokane's geology. Life had been interrupted for just a week.

In retrospect, 1980 may also be seen as the beginning of a series of manmade cataclysms that shook Spokane more profoundly. The attempt to put Spokane on the right track by sprucing it up through Expo was immediately undermined by fundamental changes in the national and world economy.

Those railroad tracks that Spokane leaders took such joy in removing represented, after all, Spokane's rationale

Terry Novak, city manager of Spokane 1978-1991. When complete consolidation of city and county governments appeared unlikely, Novak solved many local government duplication and coordination problems by arranging working agreements with the county and other towns. Courtesy, The Spokesman-Review

for being. If Spokane was not a crossroads, what was it? There were the traditional industries—agriculture, mining and lumber—but in the early 1980s all three went into a slide. In 1983, unemployment in Spokane was an incredible 12 percent, and those employed were generally earning below the statewide average.

Economic changes contributed to the disappearance of many Spokane fixtures in the 1980s. Locally-owned financial institutions that had been stalwarts of

The interior of the historic Davenport Hotel. Photo by Richard Heinzen

Expo—Lincoln Savings, Old National Bank, Fidelity Savings, and others—disappeared in merger frenzy. The Davenport Hotel closed in 1986, and for the rest of the century Spokane's palace teetered between destruction and resurrection. The Spokane *Chronicle*, part of Spokane afternoons for over a century, folded into the *Spokesman-Review*. Penney's Department store, kept downtown by extraordinary efforts of William Cowles, 3rd after Expo, moved to the suburbs a decade later, after all.

The Crescent Department Store had been Spokane's symbol of the material goods of American life. Its vast oak and green chambers displayed counters loaded with jewelry, watches and redolent perfumes, rows upon rows of suits, piles of sweaters, carousels laden with dresses, a coffee shop and two restaurants, a bookstore, a vast toy department, sofas in leather or satin, electronic gadgets, fine chinaware and silverware to launch new marriages, drapes, records, and shoes. At Christmas the store's windows at Main and Wall were cleared of elegant mannequins and replaced with a winter tableau of falling snow, reindeer, animated elves, and Santa. In 1988, after 99 years as the Crescent, the store was renamed Frederick and Nelson. It closed under that name four years later.

A decade after Expo, Spokane business leaders decided they needed to start all over again. The aim this time was not downtown renewal but something even more ambitious. They decided Spokane's economy had to be remade so that it would not be as vulnerable to economic downturns, and to provide more and better jobs.

David Clack of the Old National Bank hosted a general meeting of local leaders

Spokane's historic Crescent department store closing down. The store's clock, here marking its final minutes, was familiar to nearly everyone in Spokane. "Meet me under the Crescent clock" was a common arrangement for people having to make contact downtown. The store got its name from its first location where Riverside curved into Monroe, forming a crescent-shaped store frontage at the east side of The Spokesman-Review building. The store later moved to Riverside and Wall. The Crescent opened in 1889 and closed, under its recent name change, Frederick and Nelson, in 1992. Courtesy, The Spokesman-Review

at the Red Lion Inn in the Spokane Valley, January 4–6, 1987. One hundred and ten business, government, labor and education leaders agreed to form an organization called Momentum, to be financed by donations from the business community. The four chairmen were Clack, *Spokesman-Review* publisher William Cowles, 3rd, Paul A. Redmond,

chief executive officer of Washington Water Power Company, and Lewis G. Zirkle, president of Key Tronic, Spokane's first major company in the new computer industry.

For the next 10 years, volunteers gathered information, made contacts with industries all over the country, attended untold numbers of committee meetings, and donated millions of dollars to support the effort. At the end of that period they counted 37,000 new jobs to the area, including those in new plants built by such national firms as Boeing Aircraft and BF Goodrich Company. Momentum also conceived and brought to fruition the SIRTI new business "incubator," the Spokane Higher Education Center to increase advanced learning in the city, and the Agricultural Trade Center, which put Spokane in contention for national conventions.

By 1997 unemployment in Spokane had dropped to about the state average. But jobs in Spokane still paid less. Spokane's after-tax income was 16 percent less than the state as a whole. Per capita income was 12 percent less than the national average. A national consulting firm hired by Momentum to

William Cowles, 3rd, publisher of The Spokesman-Review *from 1970 until his death of a heart attack in 1992. He was a key figure in both Expo and Momentum, as well as the pivotal donor to the Centennial Trail and dozens of other Spokane charities and causes. During the same period he restored and expanded the Spokesman-Review Building and the Chronicle Building and completely revamped his newspaper. Courtesy, Cowles Publishing*

Gonzaga students fly a kite on a campus playfield. Condominiums and downtown Spokane are in the background. Courtesy, The Spokesman-Review

Patsy Clark's is the most well known of the Kirkland Cutter homes in Spokane and is one of the several that turn 100 this year. Photo by Kristy MacDonald. Courtesy, The Spokesman Review

assess the situation turned in a dour report. It said Spokane's public leadership was weak, the downtown was still deteriorating, and researchers were "astonished at the level of poverty in this community." It was not the kind of report Momentum wanted to hear after a decade of hard work.

Many Momentum initiatives had made no impact on the local economy because they were never tried. Again and again through the 1980s and 1990s, Momentum had offered plans aimed at reviving the economy, only to see them rejected by voters who had to approve a modest tax to support them.

The history of Spokane's Arena illustrated the business community's frustration. Three bond campaigns to raise the money, each requiring tremendous volunteer efforts, failed by large margins. Finally, in the manner that was so common during Expo, Spokane leaders went to the state legislature and obtained special legislation so that Spokane could use a hotel room tax to back bonds for the self-supporting facility.

Even as the Arena was finally opening that fall of 1995, voters went to the polls and rejected two other Mo-

mentum-backed initiatives, city-county government consolidation and addition of a Science Center to Riverfront Park.

The failed Science Center became a symbol of Spokane's problem. It was modeled upon a tested and highly successful program in Seattle. Private doners, including the Cowles family, offered to put up much of the initial investment. The center would need some tax support in the short run, but sponsors made a good case that it would eventually be self-supporting. The Park Board and city council both gave enthusiastic endorsements.

But as had happened so many times before, a small group of opponents collected the requisite number of signatures and forced an election. By just 350 votes out of 30,000 cast, the Science Center failed. The heart of the park at the heart of the city remained devoted to kiddy rides and pinball machines.

Jim Ray, a former IBM executive who became a civic hero through his tireless work to build the Arena, published an open letter that vented the frustrations of most of Spokane's leadership. He excoriated those who used referendums to defeat projects like the Arena and Science Center, "purveyors of distrust, misconception and fear. . . . obstructionists who never offer realistic alternatives or visions."

Ray continued: "We have a bunch of sheep around here when it comes to elections. Whenever any naysayers start questioning good things, they get right on board." With that passage Ray added a new term to Spokane's political lexicon —"naysayers." He also raised the most puzzling question of that era: why would voters "get right on board" and defeat "good things?"

In 1987, the year Momentum began its efforts, two political scientists at Eastern Washington University took a careful look at this question. Robert Herold and George Durrie concluded that, though it was true Spokane had many apathetic and apolitical citizens, Spokane's problems could be traced to a system of government that had shallow roots in the community. With no formal recruitment system, running for office was likely to be a matter of insiders tapping other insiders. Elections in which all citizens voted for all council members blurred the connection between representative and represented. In office, council members were hampered in winning the loyalty of their supporters by the fact that the daily operations of city government were reserved for the city manager and major initiatives were usually in the hands of business. Leaders who have little opportunity to help followers also tend to have little influence over them. Spokane had developed a system of leadership, Herold summarized later, that was good at putting together deals at the top, but which lacked the deep roots that would bring along the

Jim Chase, mayor 1981-1985. Courtesy, Northwest Room, Spokane Public Library

rest of the population.

Of course, the business community that introduced the city manager system had answers for every one of those criticisms. Representation by district tended to make council members sensitive to their own districts but not to the welfare of the whole city. A strong

Riverfront Park served the purpose envisioned for it by the designers of Expo—a beautiful and relaxing refuge at the center of a busy city. Photo by Richard Heinzen

The Spokane Falls from the footbridge adjacent to the Upper Falls Power Plant. Photo by Colin Mulvany. Courtesy, The Spokes-man-Review

Bottom right: Mayor Sheri Barnard. Courtesy, Sheri Barnard

Vicki McNeill, first female mayor, 1985-1989. Courtesy, Northwest Room, Spokane Public Library

mayor system was likely to replace a citizen-mayor and a professionally trained manager with a professional politician and his brother-in-law. In general, a more politicized system would sacrifice a culture that fosters cooperation among diverse interests.

But business leaders had heard this warning before. One of the first things Expo organizer King Cole noticed about Spokane when he arrived in 1963, he would later tell Expo historian William Youngs, was that "there was a lack of public participation" in Spokane projects. Cole told Spokane business leaders, "We're marching alone. There's nobody behind us."

Cole surprised the business leaders who had hired him by launching his efforts to revive downtown in the local neighborhoods. With the help of Mayor Fosseen, Cole spent a year encouraging formation of a broad-based citizens group that became Associations for a Better Community (ABC). It was comprised of representatives of 152 local

organizations, including the American Legion, Camp Fire Girls, Civic Theater, Spokane Taxpayers Association and Spokane's garden clubs. They talked about all sorts of projects such as teenage recreation programs, street

improvement, creation of a zoo, and the like.

ABC introduced many citizens to the idea of participation in local affairs. Spokane's first African American mayor, Jim Chase, attended ABC meetings as a representative of the National Association for the Advancement of Colored People (NAACP). He was elected to the city council after Expo and followed Ron Bair as mayor in 1981. A friendly man who could lighten the mood in a room simply by entering it, Chase might have been an effective ambassador to groups suspicious of downtown leadership. And Spokane citizens might have been won over. In this supposed era of "naysayers" of the 1980s and '90s, Spokane citizens had said yes to replacing or renovating every school, every library, and every fire station in the city.

But the leadership potential of James Chase was seldom called upon. Spokane had long since honed a two-track form of leadership. The business community, represented by the Chamber of Commerce, advocated large projects and economic development. City government handled the mundane tasks of delivering services unless it got business's call for help. Since the city was always strapped for funds, mayors and councils could initiate only modest social programs, generally using grants. Mayor Chase's legacy, the Chase Youth Commission, was the kind of social endeavor which, though it might be nice, made little impact on the imaginations of business leaders.

A dozen years later, business took a fresh look at the significance of programs for youth. In its ambitious inquiry into potential routes to economic salvation, Momentum discovered that one thing was linked to another until the elements of economic development reached well beyond economics. A key to bringing businesses to Spokane, for example, was

an educated workforce. That not only meant good schools, but also young people motivated to attend them. Thus, one of Momentum's listed goals was to ensure that every child have at least one adult in his or her life who provided meaningful guidance.

But what was the business community supposed to do with such a far-reaching social goal? At the end of its nine-year run, Momentum simply commended the social goals to the rest of the community. Meanwhile, it invested in a new organization, Focus 21, to pursue economic development more strictly defined.

Mayor Chase's political instincts and ideas contributed little to business' aim of improving the city, while at the same time businesses' great resources were detached from the very kinds of things, like youth commissions, that touched most people directly. This disconnect was one of the most important sources of Spokane's deepening divisions.

Jim Chase's successor, Vicki McNeil, was the city's first female mayor. A gracious woman who entered city government out of the best civic motives, she spent much of her time in office acting as a breakwater to furious protests by citizens suspicious of business initiatives.

Her successor, Sheri Barnard, ran for office as an opponent of a proposed $300 million trash incinerator that was high on Momentum's to-do list. For the first time, the business community faced the prospect of a mayor opposed to its program. A political consultant hired by the Washington Water Power Company reported, in a confidential memorandum, that voter opinion was divided on building the waste plant, but solidly against building it at the proposed site near the airport. The memo said that no other concern, not even the economy and crime, rivaled voter interest in the issue. The issue would probably be seen as a "referendum" on the waste plant. The memorandum said, "business' preferred candidate for Mayor," Councilman Rob Higgins was not likely to beat the very popular Barnard. However, it went on, with large amounts of money and a campaign that emphasized Barnard's faults, "this election can still be won."

Won by whom? Ironically the business community that had championed non-partisan, at-large elections to get petty politics out of local government had found itself forming a virtual political party, agreeing on a program, recruiting candidates for public office, and giving them campaign support. It appeared to be the only way to get their projects through if every initiative was going to be met by powerful opposition. When the secret political memorandum was leaked to the press it practically guaranteed Barnard's election.

Spokane politics had entered a polarizing cycle in which the defensive moves of those trying to get projects

done were the very moves that produced more suspicions. A young architect who arrived in Spokane in the early 1990s, Rick Hastings, thought Spokane could be the "Vienna of the West" if it developed its riverfront wisely. He was disappointed to hear that the city planned to build a bridge across the crest of the falls. He thought a bridge would block sunlight from the fulminating water and replace the roar of the water with the roar of truck tires.

But he heard no one questioning the bridge. Downtown business leaders, who had the most to lose if the city center's great natural attraction was degraded, seemed comfortable with the bridge. The *Spokesman-Review* editorial page was positively rhapsodic about the advantages of a new bridge. Hastings could only assume that before he arrived all the alternatives to the bridge had been searched out and found unsatisfactory.

Then Hastings read a short article in The *Inlander*, Spokane's weekly newspaper launched in 1993 by Ted

Spokane's Higher Education Center, which opened in 1996, expanded the Spokane presence of both Washington State University and Eastern Washington University. Courtesy, Higher Education Center

McGreggor. The article raised the same questions about the bridge that had occurred to Hastings. Hastings started talking to others about the bridge and discovered they were not so much convinced the bridge was a good thing as that it would be a bad thing to question it. The reasoning seemed to be that if The *Spokesman-Review* was for it, then it must mean that it was essential to River Park Square, the new mall being developed by the owners of the newspaper. Few people who worried about the future of the downtown wanted to stand in the way of that project.

Two other relative newcomers to the city, attorneys Doug and Laurel Siddoway, joined Hastings' opposition to the bridge and soon discovered the same problem. The city's rationale for the bridge was highly debatable, but try to debate it, said Doug Siddoway, and others wrote you off as a "Birkenstock-wearing, Cowles-hating, Luddite." Siddoway concluded that the city's political culture was "anemic" and unable to sustain the normal give-and-take of political discussion.

The bridge opponents, joined by Spokane physician and former legislator John Moyer, took their case to the state's Department of Ecology, which halted the bridge on the grounds that it violated the Shorelines Protection Act and the city had not proved a need for it.

Whether Spokane needed a bridge or not, it was an embarrassment that an agency on the other side of the state should have to make the decision. This had become something of a pattern. The official organization chart of Spokane's city governmental process showed a neat line of authority from the policy-making council to execution by the city manager. But a chart that reflected the reality of the 1990s would have added a tangle of messy lines flowing from the council to appeals to other levels of government, to referendum elections, and to the courts.

The First Avenue law office of Stephen Eugster became an unofficial headquarters to resisters of City Hall. Urged on by many who were suspicious of city government, Eugster filed challenge after challenge to city actions. In 1995 he had five lawsuits pending against the city and more in the works. His main target was the "public-private partnership" in which the city was contributing to the development of River Park Square.

One unlikely supporter to Eugster was Paul Sandifur, Jr., president of Metropolitan Mortgage and Securities

The Centennial Trail follows the bank of the Spokane River, from Nine Mile Falls through downtown Spokane, and on to the Idaho State border. It attracts walkers, runners, bicyclists and skaters all along that route. The photo shows a section of the trail between Riverfront Park and Division Street. Photo by Christopher Anderson. Courtesy, The Spokesman-Review

University for organizing an anti-war strike among the faculty. Twenty-five years later Sandifur the financier, said he felt uncomfortable sitting in closed meetings in which important public policy was discussed. Even as the owner of major downtown properties he was not privy to the details of the agreements between the city and the developers of River Park Square. He was told these details were considered trade secrets by the Nordstrom store chain. He withdrew and became a member of an opposition that had begun to form around the issue of River Park Square.

The city of Spokane contributed to the shopping mall by purchasing the Cowles'-owned parking garage over Post Street for just under $30 million, money that was then invested in the new mall. The city also helped the developers obtain a $22 million federal loan, granted on the rationale that the development was a spur to Spokane's economic development. The Cowles invested $60 million of their own funds in the development.

The plan had wide support among Spokane leadership. Mayor Jack Geraghty led a city council that steadily supported the city's participation with 7-0 votes.

Eugster, Sandifur and many others called it "corporate welfare," the use of scarce enough federal and local funds to help a rich developer. But their core argument was that the city had concentrated its resources in the wrong industry. Shopping and convention business would create mostly low-paid clerk and waiter jobs. Meanwhile, they argued, the future was passing Spokane by. *Forbes* magazine, a national economics publication, had ranked Spokane as one of the least attractive places in the country for high tech companies to do business. "People in this city are poor," argued John Stone, a Spokane contractor

Company, a national firm headquartered in Spokane and one of the city's major businesses. Spokane politics had always had dissenters, but seldom any among wealthy downtown property owners.

Perhaps there was a hint of generational differences in these arguments. The Expo model was created by people shaped in World War II and by Spokane's hard-scrabble days of the '30s, '40s and '50s. To them, cooperation was not something nice to have, but rather a requirement imposed by outside dangers. Sandifur was formed by a different tradition. Though a banker in the 1990s, he was a protestor against the Vietnam War in the 1960s. He was thrown out of San Francisco State

and one of those arguing with the city's participation in River Park Square. "You can see it in the clothes they wear and the cars they drive. This is the best economy this country has ever seen, and Spokane is missing it." Stone organized a series of seminars on the question of how Spokane could increase its appeal to high-tech industries.

Eugster challenged the city's participation in River Park Square all the way to the Washington State Supreme Court, which found that the Spokane City Council had acted within its rights in passing the necessary ordinances as "emergencies," thus blocking the possibility of a referendum vote. Later the state's auditor added another outside opinion. He said the agreement between the developers and the city was "creative," but nevertheless quite legal. He went on to criticize the Spokane City Council, however, for blocking a public vote. "The debate should have been welcomed, particularly for such a large-scale

project. The feeling that citizens were left out of the debate only heightened suspicions over the creative course the city took to assist in the project."

The city council wanted to block a public vote for fear downtown renewal would become a whipping boy for the proliferating complaints against the city. But there was a mayoral election coming up in 1997. One of the council's most persistent critics, John Talbott, announced he would run for mayor and make the election a virtual referendum on River Park Square. Talbott, a retired Air Force colonel, had returned to his hometown of Spokane to become a neighborhood volunteer. He soon found he objected to the chummy politics of Spokane's establishment.

On the eve of the mayoral election between Geraghty and Talbott, Stacey Cowles, the publisher of the *Spokesman-Review*, wrote an appeal to the public in his newspaper. That he should do so was, in the long view of Spokane history,

The Spokane Veterans Memorial Arena, which opened in August 1995, replaced the 40-year-old Coliseum. It seats over 12,000 and was designed by ACLS Architects of Spokane. Garco Construction of Spokane was the general contractor. Photo by Christopher Anderson. Courtesy, The Spokesman-Review

133

Mayor John Talbott. Courtesy, Office of the Mayor

The Spokane Chiefs play hockey in the Veterans Memorial Arena. Photo by Colin Mulvany. Courtesy, The Spokesman-Review

itself an extraordinary event. The Cowles family had been intimately involved in Spokane's politics, business and charities for over a century, but always managed to do so while keeping a low profile.

"We knew," Cowles wrote, "that we could face damage to our credibility as a news institution over perceived conflict of interest on the River Park Square story—[and] we were going to have to compromise a century of tradition and give up a degree of privacy long cherished by our families. It would have been so much easier to quit, and close up the buildings."

"Yes, a successful downtown will provide some benefit to my company's business—as well as all of the other businesses downtown. A successful downtown also will bring fresh cash to the city treasury, avoid the costly problems of urban decay, keep Spokane's image attractive, help provide more exciting opportunities

for our children and provide a base for healthy growth throughout our region."

Talbott was elected by 433 votes out of 57,337 cast. The city was divided right down the middle.

After the election, the downtown business community and the Chamber of Commerce operated as much as possible as if Spokane did not have a mayor. But the city did have a mayor, and Talbott made his presence known when he refused to endorse an effort to get state help in expanding Spokane's Convention Center. Downtown boosters were appalled. The Convention Center at the east end of downtown was envisioned as the other part of the River Park Square plan to keep Spokane a regional destination.

In the final year of the century, exactly 25 years after Expo, the issues appeared headed toward some kind of resolution.

River Park Square opened on August 20, 1999, a city block and four levels of sparkling stores, theaters, and restaurants. People were impressed. It demonstrated what Spokane's traditional business leadership could accomplish.

Meanwhile, all the critics of that tradition prepared to make their point in the elections that fall. One ballot item would change Spokane's form of government to the strong mayor system. Another would require that citizens have a chance to vote before any new bridges were built across the river. Gadfly attorney Stephen Eugster and Steve Corker, the public relations executive who led the campaign against the Science Center in 1995, both announced they would run against council members who had supported River Park Square.

Perhaps just as significant, at least two representatives of Spokane's neighborhood councils ran for city council in that election. They repre-

sented grass-roots constituencies that might break the deadlock between downtown factions. Al French, an architect and president of the Lidgerwood Neighborhood Council, led his neighborhood to winning a national award for collaborations between community and business. He ran for council, not for or against downtown projects, but on a "bring the city together" platform.

One morning that summer of 1999, Neal Fosseen, still on the job at age 91, was in his office on the 14th floor of the Old National Bank Building. The north-facing window of the office looked out on a resplendent Spokane morning in Riverfront Park, where people walked, biked, and chased after their children, exactly as Fosseen and other leaders had envisioned four decades earlier.

Fosseen was discussing Spokane's politics when his phone rang. "Yes, Stacey," Fosseen said into the phone, and then arranged the time of his monthly luncheon with the publisher of The *Spokesman-Review*, the fourth generation of Cowles he had known personally. Soon the phone rang again. "Hello, Paul," he said. It was the president of Metropolitan Mortgage and Securities, Paul Sandifur, Jr. Fosseen, in many ways the essence of Spokane's old-club way of doing things, and Sandifur, the rebel against it, were, it turned out, not only close friends, but great admirers of each other.

Fosseen's next appointment arrived at his office door. It was Al French of the Lidgerwood neighborhood, come to consult with the Mayor. One of Spokane's oldest leaders and one of its newest sat down to talk about the city's future.

In that last summer and autumn of the 20th century, the next chapter of Spokane's history was anything but clear. But the people of Spokane were settling into the task of writing it.

The Spokane Falls and Monroe Street Bridge from the air, 1999. Photo by Christopher Anderson. Courtesy, The Spokesman-Review

CHRONICLES OF LEADERSHIP

Facing page: *Thomas F. Conlan and A.P. Wolverton organized the Spokane Hardware Company in January of 1886. Conlan, standing with his back to the camera, bought out Wolverton in 1888 and remained with the company until 1910. In 1892, a year before this photo, Conlan built this two-story building to house his store on Riverside Avenue, west of the Sherwood Building. (EWSHS)*

The history of business is an important aspect of Spokane's past. Commerce and industry helped make Spokane a city and the economic center of a vast intermountain hinterland.

In every large community new businesses are formed almost daily. Only a few survive, and they acquire economic strength that affects not only the lives and well-being of owners, employees, and customers, but also of the city as a whole. If business is not the heart, the soul, or the mind of the community, it is at least its lifeblood.

Three moments in Spokane's history seem to have been especially propitious for business formation. Early opportunities arose during Spokane's growth years, particularly in the decade after the fire when new construction and a surging population transformed a frontier settlement into an important Western city. During this period Spokane became an established financial, transportation, and distribution center.

After World War I Spokane's period of rapid growth was replaced by a more tempered pace of business activity and then, in concert with the nation, economic depression. World War II and New Deal spending helped to reverse the decline, and Spokane entered a second phase of significant growth and new business formation in the decade following 1945.

The plateau that was reached in the sixties provided a solid foundation for a revival of business activity in the seventies. Shaken from complacency, Spokane's business leaders embraced an enthusiasm that was reflected both in Expo '74 and in the spate of high-tech business starts that link Spokane industry to the future.

What transformations the future will bring are difficult to predict. Major changes in Spokane-area business and industry have already occurred, such as a diminished role for Northwest forest products and farms that can produce food in abundance but only wafer-thin margins of profit. Other natural-resource industries, such as mining and electric power generation, remain important—but no longer demand the legions of employees that made Spokane a destination for job-hungry workers in years past.

The changes of tomorrow are occurring now, gradually and often silently. Spokane, once proud to be the hub of the Inland Empire, increasingly looks beyond its backyard to the marketplace of the world.

Today businesses of all kinds flourish in Spokane. Some are industry leaders in advanced-technology fields. Others perform more traditional tasks in banking, retailing, and manufacturing. Still others provide services, such as education, medical care, and communication.

Many are the businesses that have helped to shape Spokane. Those whose stories appear on the following pages have chosen to support the publication of this book. In this way they have contributed to making the history of Spokane—including that of its businesses—a resource for the future.

ALLIED SECURITY INTERNATIONAL

Who would believe it?

One of the country's largest full-service security equipment companies located right here in Spokane Falls?

ALLIED SECURITY, located at 2nd & Stevens, now in its third generation of Hunt family ownership traces its origin back to 1902—then known as Spokane Safe & Lock Company.

Allied's "modern" era began in 1948 when R.A. (Bob) Hunt, owner of the R.A. Hunt Advertising Agency, purchased Spokane Safe & Lock Company from Arthur (Art) Duncan, the owner and operator since 1936. In 1948, the "shop" as it was called, was located next to the old Eagles Lodge at S. 176 Howard Street and had five employees who sold, installed and serviced small safes,

Allied's Spokane office in 1966.

locks and keys throughout the Spokane area.

Bob Hunt's goal was to grow the business beyond the Inland Empire and broaden the base of sales and service to include security products to banks and other financial institutions. The first step was taken in 1952 with the acquisition of the Portland Safe Company, which led to the decision in 1953 to incorporate in the State of Washington under the

Allied's founder, Robert A. Hunt.

name "Allied Safe & Vault Co." The next step was to move the Spokane office to larger quarters at S. 211 Howard Street.

In 1954, the oldest of Bob and Cora's two sons, Robin Hunt, began working in the business while attending Eastern Washington University. After graduating, Robin served in the U.S. Army from 1961 to 1981, retiring as a Lt. Colonel.

In 1957, their youngest son, Terrill (Terry), was employed by Allied (Spokane Safe & Lock Company) and in the same year a sales and service outlet opened in Seattle, operating as "Allied Safe & Vault—Seattle."

Allied, through its offices in Portland, Seattle and Spokane was rapidly becoming one of the West's larger distributors in security equipment and services. In 1966, the corporate headquarters of Allied Safe & Vault Co. and the retail Spokane Safe & Lock Company moved to their present location at 2nd & Stevens in Spokane.

A significant event in the early 1970s was Allied's entry into the manufacture of bank security equipment. Allied constructed a

large, steel, walk-in vault provided to the State of Montana at no charge for use during EXPO '74, to store a valuable collection of Charlie Russell's original paintings.

In 1976, Terry Hunt was named president of Allied.

The 1980s proved to be exciting and also sad. Allied's 24-hour alarm monitoring center was established in Spokane in 1980. Some time later, an alliance was formed with the Alarm Monitoring Center in Lacey, Washington to monitor alarms out of Allied's Boise, Portland and Seattle offices.

Taking another huge step in 1981, Allied purchased the Gary Safe Company, a manufacturer of security safes with plants in Los Angeles and Cincinnati, Ohio.

Overnight Allied had grown from a $15 million company with about 50 employees to a $25 million company with 150 employees. About this time Robin Hunt retired from the military to join forces with his father and brother and in 1982 was named President

Robin R. Hunt as a locksmith in 1954.

HE'S A "KEY MAN." That generally is pretty good. Robin Hunt's a key man in fact. He makes duplicates and he's never been locked out.

Terry E. Hunt, CEO and president, and his wife, Roberta.

of the newly acquired "Allied-Gary Safe Company." Shortly thereafter, Gary Safe's Los Angeles plant was consolidated with Allied's manufacturing plant located in Spokane.

Unfortunately, the saddest day was in 1985 when the founder and father, Bob Hunt passed away.

In 1987, the third generation of Hunts, Terry's son Jay joined the business, working out of the Boise office until moving to Spokane in 1992. Jay currently serves as vice

Jay Hunt, vice-president and Spokane general manager.

president and general manager of Allied's Spokane retail branch.

Allied-Spokane was deeply involved in the manufacture of security equipment for banks and financial institutions (vault doors, safe deposit boxes, drive-up systems, night depositories, etc.) and security cash safes, including electronically-controlled cash dispensers (the "Autobank") for use by convenience stores. However, in the 1990s, Allied's direction focused more towards the sales,

1953 Spokane Lilac parade float.

installation and service of electronic alarm security, CCTV, access control and fire alarm systems.

In addition, profit margins from bank equipment sales were eroding due to competitive pressures from low-cost imports from Japan, China and Korea.

By 1991, all "Allied-Gary" manufacturing plants—including Spokane—had been consolidated into a 100,000 square-foot facility located just south of Augusta, Georgia.

In order to concentrate resources and fulfill Allied's

mission of being the premier security company in the Northwest, a decision was made to sell the manufacturing subsidiary—the Gary Safe Company.

Since the sale of the subsidiary in 1997, ALLIED SECURITY currently consists of corporate headquarters and a retail branch in Spokane, and branches in Boise, Portland and Seattle, employing 150 people with a total estimated annual payroll of $4.6 million. (Spokane has 52 people and annual payroll of $1.6 million).

One of the notable hallmarks of Allied since its inception has been a commitment to community involvement. Bob Hunt began this tradition with his active participation and leadership in numerous service organizations. This tradition continues to be followed by family and employees alike. As an example, Bob Hunt and his son Terry have the distinction of being the only father-son combination to have served as president of the Inland Northwest Boy Scout Council. Jay Hunt is currently a vice president of the Council.

And finally—special recognition must be given to all those employees of Spokane Safe & Lock Company and ALLIED SECURITY—past and present.

Allied's success could not have been possible without the dedication and loyalty of these hardworking individuals—especially Mr. Max Kirklin, a Spokane-native now working out of the Portland office, who celebrates his 50th year with Allied in 1999.

COLUMBIA LIGHTING

A German immigrant named Rudolph Doerr left Pennsylvania in late 1897 to come to Spokane, then a rapidly growing community of some 30,000 people. Once here, he set up shop with local electrician, Joseph R. Mitchell. Doerr, Mitchell and Company was originally located on the southeast corner of 1st and Howard, a site now occupied, coincidentally, by the Columbia Building. The company was a primary supplier of electrical and gas supplies, "Chandeliers and Gasoline Lamps, Telephones, etc." In 1936, then known as the Brown-Johnston Company, the company moved into the Armour Building on Wall Street to provide more space for the expanding business and to begin manufacturing fixtures for the new technology of fluorescent lighting. The owner at that time was the prominent Eric A. Johnston, nationally known for his involvement in business, government, diplomacy, and the arts. Johnston was for many years

Columbia Electric & Manufacturing, 1941.

president of the Motion Picture Association of America and served an unprecedented four years as president of the U.S. Chamber of Commerce.

The company's name was changed in 1940 to Columbia Electric and Manufacturing, but its growing fluorescent business was to be short-lived. World War II saw the conversion of Columbia's entire production to the war

Doerr-Mitchell & Co., First & Howard, 1897.

effort. In its support of the U.S. Navy and U.S. Army, the company manufactured over 600 different items, including more than 12 million 200mm and 81mm projectile casings.

With the end of the war, the cancellation of defense contracts left Columbia scrambling to keep its workforce busy. Nearly a million mailboxes built from surplus aluminum, and large lighting contracts for Shasta and Grand Coulee Dams aided a successful adjustment to a peacetime economy.

After the war, the company focused its efforts on the design and manufacture of custom fluorescent fixtures. In the late 1950s Columbia developed a line of high-end recessed fluorescent troffers using Corning glass. This line, and a successful custom business, allowed Columbia to become an industry leader in the fluorescent lighting market.

The year 1966 marked a major turning point for Columbia. The company embarked on a major

program of product expansion, resulting in the development and introduction of the Parabolume series of parabolic fixtures in the fall of that year. As the industry's first parabolic troffer, it was one of the single most important developments in lighting over the past 40 years. The fixture was designed to control and distribute light in a predetermined pattern. Much more efficient than traditional lensed fixtures, this new fixture also reduced glare and maintenance requirements. These advantages made the parabolic troffer the de facto standard of commercial lighting to the present day.

Columbia Lighting continued to expand its offering of parabolic troffers and other fluorescent products over the next several years. In 1981, Columbia became part of U.S. Industries. In 1992, 95 years after Rudolph Doerr left Pennsylvania, Columbia Lighting returned to absorb Keystone Lighting, a Philadelphia-area manufacturer of commodity fluorescent lighting. With Keystone marketed under the Columbia name, Columbia Lighting was able to offer a full-spectrum of fluorescent lighting for every phase of the commercial business.

After more than 100 years of growth, Columbia Lighting has become the third largest fluorescent lighting manufacturer in North America. Headquartered in Spokane, Columbia has an additional manufacturing facility in Bristol, Pennsylvania, and an extensive network of warehouses and distribution centers throughout the U.S. and Canada. A division of Lighting Corporation of America, the company employs over 1,400 people nationwide, and over 600 in Spokane alone, under the guidance of its president, Robert H. Ingram.

Columbia Lighting, present-day headquarters in Spokane's Industrial Park.

Columbia products are marketed through electrical distributors to the electrical contractor, and are installed in a variety of buildings such as schools, hospitals, office buildings, and libraries. Naturally, Columbia Lighting fixtures are found throughout the greater Spokane area. Installations include the Federal, Seafirst, Paulsen, IBM, Avista, and ONB buildings, the Metropolitan Financial Center, the New City Hall, and several Safeway,

Brown-Johnston Company, 1928.

Albertson's, Tidyman's and Rosauer's grocery stores.

Columbia's high-performance library stack fixtures can be found at the Spokane Public Library, the Whitworth Library, Washington State University's Holland Library, Eastern Washington University's JFK Library, and Gonzaga's Foley Law Library. Columbia Lighting is also prominent in indirect fluorescent lighting; a 1995 project at General Motors Truck product Center in Pontiac, Michigan is the largest indirect lighting installation in the country. Columbia shipped over 12 miles of extruded aluminum designer-quality fixtures in two short months.

A century-long tradition of excellence and value has made Columbia one of the lighting industry's most respected manufacturers, known for quality, performance and value.

CXT INCORPORATED

Relationships as Durable as Our Products. These are the defining words for CXT Incorporated, a leading supplier of prestressed concrete railroad products and precast concrete buildings based in Spokane since 1987. CXT's strength and success are rooted in a commitment to building solid relationships with employees, customers, suppliers and the Spokane community.

CXT History: CXT originated from Con-Force Costain Concrete Tie Co. Ltd., a Canadian company that was formed as a joint venture in 1973 between Con-Force Products of Calgary, Canada and Costain Concrete Limited, England—a major supplier of concrete track ties to British Rail. As a result of this joint venture, a tie plant was constructed in Edmonton, Canada in 1975 that produced more than four million ties before closing in 1990. During this time, the British company Costain Concrete Limited became sole owners of the company. In 1986, the company name changed

CXT employs a skilled work force of experts in the business of making concrete ties and other concrete products.

to CXT—the name it holds today. It stands for *Concrete Cross Ties.*

With a growing North American concrete tie market, the management and employees of CXT made a bold move in 1990 and purchased the U.S. company from Costain through an Employee Stock Ownership Plan (ESOP).

The next 10 years brought significant growth to CXT's concrete railroad products' markets, meanwhile the company diversified into new products, including a line of precast concrete buildings.

In June 1999 CXT's employee shareholders approved the sale of CXT to the L.B. Foster Company—a manufacturer, fabricator and distributor of rail and track-work, piling, highway products, earth wall systems and tubular products—in a move designed to secure future growth for the company and its product lines. As an L.B. Foster Company, CXT (now organized into two divisions: Concrete Railroad Products and Precast Concrete Products) and its more than 265 employees gained a vast distribution network and the investment capital necessary to facilitate growth well into the 21st century.

CXT Concrete Railroad Products Division: CXT's Concrete Railroad Products Division produces high-quality concrete railroad products in use on main line, short line, commuter and transit railroads as well as port and industrial track systems throughout the United States, Canada and Puerto Rico. CXT's comprehensive line of railroad products includes: track ties, turnout ties, guard rail ties, gantry crane ties, specialty ties, and grade crossing systems.

The core business of CXT's railroad products group is concrete track ties. In fact, since 1973, CXT has produced more than nine million concrete ties—more than all of its U.S. and Canadian competitors combined. Ties are produced from two tie plants: one in Spokane and another located in Grand Island, Nebraska.

The Spokane Tie Plant was built in 145 days between early November 1986 and mid-March 1987—a local record for speed of construction. The plant occupies 55,000 square-feet and was built in response to an order from Burlington Northern Railroad

CXT precast toilet buildings are virtually indestructible and arrive preassembled and ready to install.

More than 9 million CXT concrete ties are in use throughout the United States, Canada and Puerto Rico. Courtesy, Union Pacific Museum Collection

(BN) to make 1.75 million concrete ties over a five-year period. Since that time, CXT has produced concrete track ties, turnout ties and grade crossing systems for Union Pacific Railroad, Burlington Northern Santa Fe, Canadian Pacific Railroad, and CN Railroad, as well as track systems in Baltimore, San Diego, Los Angeles, Denver, Calgary, Edmonton, Portland, Salt Lake City, New Jersey and Puerto Rico.

The Grand Island Tie Plant, a segmental plant designed and patented by CXT, was also constructed in near-record time in 1998 within approximately 100 days between ground-breaking and the first day of production. The Grand Island plant was built in response to a five-year contract with Union Pacific Railroad to produce a minimum of 1.1 million ties for new and existing projects throughout the Union Pacific Midwest corridor.

Known for quality, durability and safety, CXT retains a staff of experienced engineers who know and understand the railroad business and the inherent benefits of prestressed concrete. Experience and a passion to continually deliver product solutions that enhance safety, durability and long-term customer investment, ensure CXT's leadership position in the continued development of the nation's railroad transportation infrastructure.

CXT Precast Concrete Products Division: CXT's Precast Concrete Products Division produces a complete line of toilet buildings used extensively by the United States Forest Service and state and county parks. One of the largest of these buildings, the Big Bear, weighs 28 tons and is shipped completely assembled with all plumbing and electrical equipment preinstalled at the CXT Precast Plant, a 120,000 square-foot manufacturing facility. All toilet buildings–offered in single vault, double vault, flush and compost styles–are delivered ready-to-use.

In addition to toilet buildings, CXT also manufactures Easi-Set buildings that have a mono-pitch roof and are a popular choice for telecommunication, pump and other utility use, as well as hazardous materials storage.

CXT precast toilet buildings meet ADA requirements and are typically constructed with steel-reinforced concrete with tamper proof components. These buildings are tough enough to stand up to the abuse of vandals and Mother Nature. Aesthetically pleasing designs are made to blend with any environment and are available in a variety of earthtone-colors with simulated barnwood or stucco finish walls and simulated shake or ribbed steel roof in concrete.

A Community Partner: Since arriving in Spokane in 1987, CXT has been and continues to be a proud community leader. As a friend to Spokane, CXT has donated resources to help with projects such as the Centennial Trail, Plantes Ferry Park, United Way, the "Climb Mt. Spokane for Your Heart" event to benefit The Heart Institute, the Economic Development Council and many others.

The Spokane Tie Plant manufactures more than 1,400 ties per day using 72 tons of cement, 350 tons of aggregate, 55 miles of wire and 5,600 shoulders for fastening systems.

DEALERS AUTO AUCTION OF SPOKANE

It's 9:00 a.m. on a typical Thursday morning, and the auction lanes at Dealers Auto Auction (DAA) of Spokane are heating up. A stream of late-model vehicles flows from a massive parking lot behind the west plains facility and into a long, low building. Volkswagen's new Beetles queue up with Jeep Grand Cherokees, and Suburbans, Cadillacs and Mercedes with Ford pickups.

To the untrained eye, the auction-room floor seems to be in perpetual chaos, but in fact, order reigns. Vehicles slip into eight auction lanes and are surrounded by bidders. Eight auctioneers, one per lane, stand in podiums above the crowd calling for bids in the rapid-fire language of the auction. Ringmen circulate on the floor, spotting bidders, moving the auction along. The buyers, an assortment of franchise dealer managers and independent auto dealer owners, bury their heads in auction reports and wholesale guide books, fixing the value of vehicles before they bid. They all have their own bidding style: a slender man in a plaid shirt and black jeans gives a wink; an older gentleman in a sport coat raises his index finger. It's noisy and fast and cars and trucks flow relentlessly across the auction-block. On an average auction day, 1,500-2,500 vehicles go on the block; those numbers double and more during a special sale or promotional event.

To put the auction weekly volume into perspective for unaffiliated industries and the general public, something like 240 new passenger vehicles are licensed in Spokane County in an average week. Clearly, the auction is big business. Auto auctions like DAA play a key role, but are largely invisible in the automotive industry. They provide a channel for re-

marketing high-quality, used vehicles into the consumer market. Those who use DAA's services include lending institutions, rental companies, independent and franchised auto dealers, and manufacturers such as Ford Motor Company and General Motors.

DAA is ideally positioned for the job; Spokane is at the heart of a geographic region that includes Washington, Idaho, Oregon, Montana, Utah, Nevada, Colorado,

Bob McConkey, Jr., president.

DAA boasts the newest and most modern auction facility in the Pacific Northwest.

Northern California, and Western Canada. With a robust economy and an energetic and growing workforce, the area has emerged as one of the nation's fastest-growing automotive markets. And because Spokane is a transportation hub, product is easily shipped via truck and rail throughout the United States.

Now a fixture on the west plains, Dealers Auto Auction is a young enterprise founded in 1992, when Bob McConkey, Jr. and Greg Mahugh bought the assets of a defunct Spokane auction house. Like most entrepreneurs, McConkey and Mahugh experienced lean times early on. The first sale under the DAA banner, in September 1992, wielded 34 sold of the 68 vehicles consigned, and it got worse before it got better: 16 vehicles sold at the second sale, 12 at the third.

However, McConkey and Mahugh had auctioneering in their blood. They had learned at the feet of McConkey's father, a legendary figure in northwest auction circles. Bob McConkey, Sr., his wife, Helen, and a partner co-founded the South Seattle Auto Auction in 1954, and the McConkeys held it together in the early days on pluck and wile. McConkey, Sr. is best known for issuing "insured checks," when in fact the only real insurance he could offer was his commitment to his business and its customers. In the early days he routinely chased around town hand delivering titles and personally collecting funds.

That same drive and enthusiasm saw the DAA partnership through its early days. The Big Sky Sale, DAA's first major promotional event in spring 1993 produced over 400 sold units, giving the partners their first real glimpse of the auction's potential. In spring 1996, McConkey and Mahugh launched a new five-lane facility with a party and rock 'n' roll concert featuring legendary entertainer Jerry Lee Lewis. The event was so popular that rocker Chuck Berry was hired to play the next year, and a series of popular acts has since followed.

After the first year, growth came quickly and DAA soon outgrew its building. In 1997 McConkey and Mahugh added three new auction lanes and expanded parking capacities to handle the increased consignment. Today DAA boasts the newest, most modern auction facility in the Pacific Northwest, located on over 40-black topped acres with a consignment capacity of 4,000 vehicles. In addition to the 20,000 square-foot administrative and sales facility, the complex includes an 11,000 square-foot detail shop, and a state-of-the-art paint and body shop. Plans include a full-service mechanic's shop.

Dealers Auto Auction employs a full-time staff of 160 to 200, but part-timers are critical to the

operation as well. The DAA team has been creative in finding ways to employ people who will benefit most, including retired individuals and troubled teens. DAA is involved with Teen Challenge America, a non-profit organization that incorporates Christian beliefs in a rehabilitation program that

A private concert by Jerry Lee Lewis kicked off the grand opening of DAA's new facility in 1996.

helps young people with life controlling problems to re-enter society. DAA frequently includes charitable activities in its sales. One fund-raising auction netted $59,000 for the United Way, Young Life of Spokane and the Venessa Behan Crisis Nursery. McConkey and Mahugh also often donate their time as auctioneers for local benefit auctions.

The DAA principals credit their success to two things: the company treats it's employees like family, and they in turn treat customers like friends. When the Spokane Area Chamber of Commerce honored DAA with its Agora Award for business excellence, the judges wrote: "There are auto auctions all over the country and DAA's growth has not been a matter of finding an exploding market and going along for the ride. Rather, DAA has had to grow by relying on its reputation for integrity and exemplary customer service, which accounts for the fact that it has customers from every state of the Union and Canada."

Greg Mahugh - senior vice president/ general manager

GARCO BUILDING SYSTEMS—GARCO CONSTRUCTION

Born of a humble common beginning, two companies in related, yet separate industries trace their roots to a man of uncommon vision. Wayne Garceau came home from Europe as a decorated pilot of a B-24 bomber during World War II. Upon his return, he began his career as a residential contractor on Spokane's South Hill. After a few years of building homes for the families of returning veterans, he began assembling and constructing the components for an arch-ribbed timber building used by the region's agricultural sector.

When the arch-ribbed timber laminator went out of business, Wayne decided to make use of the dealer distribution network he had established in the Inland Empire and go into manufacturing himself. He began producing an open web steel rigid frame building with wood secondary framing members. He opened the new manufacturing business at 5503 East Broadway in Spokane, while continuing to grow his construction business as a separate opera-

Garceau Steel Structures plant & office, 5503 East Broadway, Spokane, c. 1960. Photo by The Commercial Photographers

tion. The panel and trims for his new buildings were supplied by ASC Industries, just down the street from his plant. He incorporated his new company in 1958 under the name "Garceau Steel Structures," marking the beginning of Garco.

In 1967, Wayne sold part of his company to ASC Industries. By then, he had begun using steel secondary framing members, which were manufactured by ASC. This provided Garceau's customers with buildings designed and manufactured as all-steel structures.

Garceau stepped into the "big leagues" in 1971 with the development of his first solid web, built-up plate rigid frame building. It shipped to Amchitka Island in the Aleutian chain in Alaska. Built as a cable reel housing to lower a nuclear bomb test device into the ground, the building's new method of fabrication withstood a very rigorous trial. When the device was detonated, the elevation of the island dropped approximately 10'. The only damage to the building was a slide door that blew out. If ever a new product was tested under baptism by fire, this was it! No longer were Garco buildings associated with "spaghetti web, wrinkle wrap" buildings.

Gifford-Hill, a then $300 million Dallas-based public corporation focused on growth, acquired ASC Industries in 1972. With this transaction, Gifford-Hill became part owner of Garceau Steel Structures. Meanwhile, Wayne's company was growing rapidly. He had decided he needed to be a fully-integrated manufacturer of steel building systems, and that

Garco Building Systems plant & office, Airway Heights, c. 1978. Erected by Garco Construction.

Chinook Winds Casino, Lincoln City, OR. Manufactured by Garco Building Systems, 1996.

the company needed to invest heavily in more of its own equipment. This constituted a new beginning, so he also decided on a new name: Garco, Inc.

In 1976, Wayne wanted to gain back the portion of the company that Gifford-Hill had acquired. When he approached them with an offer to buy back their shares, Gifford-Hill countered by offering to buy the whole company from Wayne. The sale was consummated in June of that year and Garco, Inc. became a wholly-owned subsidiary of Gifford-Hill. This was a major milestone in the evolution of Garco. Due to the company's ongoing growth, its crowded and inefficient facility no longer supported the company's long-term efforts. A major investment in the form of a much larger and more modern facility was needed.

In May 1978, Garco Building Systems moved into its brand new facility in Airway Heights. The new plant was designed and built with the express intent of producing metal building systems, and would provide Garco the opportu-

nity to be one of the top three most efficient companies in the industry. This decision and consequent move proved to be a huge success!

Also in 1978, Tim Welsh and Bob Carter approached Gifford-Hill with a proposal to buy the Garco Construction division. Garco's then General Manager Terry Middaugh, endorsed the deal and supported Tim and Bob's effort, thereby convincing Gifford-Hill to go with the proposal. Their new company became Carter-Welsh,

Inc. doing business as Garco Construction. Tim took the reigns as the new company's president, and they were off and running.

Garco Building Systems

In their continuing drive to become a Fortune 500 company, Gifford-Hill acquired another conglomerate of about equal size and in similar industries, in December 1979. This was a poorly timed move, as the purchase was financed with a variable interest rate based on the prime rate. When their interest ballooned as high as 21.5 percent in the early 1980s, and the nation's economy slumped, the company suffered huge losses. These factors ultimately led to the sale of their remaining assets.

During this time, Pascoe Building Systems, a product of the 1979 acquisition and a competitor of Garco's, entered into the picture. Gifford-Hill's management felt it would be best to consolidate

BHP Coated Steel Corp., Kalama, WA. Manufactured by Garco Building Systems; erected by Garco Construction, 1996.

Meadow Ridge Elementary School, Mead - Garco Construction, 1992. Photo by Explosive Illusions

the Spokane firm under Pascoe's management group. These were difficult times for the local company, its employees, and its customers. Many lessons were learned during that period that have continued to serve Garco as the company grows today.

By late 1981, Gifford-Hill had hired a consulting group to advise them how to best serve their business and stockholders. From that, a recommendation was made to divest of any interests unrelated to their core business of concrete and aggregate products or sand and gravel. In April 1982, Garco was advised that the company was for sale.

General Manager Terry Middaugh worked for 18 months putting together the package that eventually allowed him to buy the assets of the business. On August 11, 1983, he acquired the former Garco, Inc. and became the new President of MIDCO Mfg., Inc., continuing business as Garco Building Systems.

Shortly following the new company's birth, Terry named his officers and hired most of the previous employees of Gifford-Hill/

Garco Building Systems' Spokane location. He then set out to introduce the "new" Garco to the former company's customers. Those first few years were difficult. Many of these contractors had moved on to nationally-based competitors or other companies that had begun to show up in the region. Eventually, though, as word got out that the "old Garco" was back, most of the customers returned, along with a host of new ones.

During the mid and late-'80s, Garco began establishing a presence in the international arena by producing large, heavy-industrial buildings for use in the mining and timber industries. This niche has continued to provide the company an identity as a well-established expert in the area of sophisticated, heavily-engineered buildings for use in a number of heavy applications. With this has come the opportunity to produce buildings for construction in such far-reaching locations such as Argentina, Chile, Russia, China, Marshall Islands, and Ghana, as well as in remote North American sites. The company maintains ongoing relationships with most of the largest engineering and construction entities in the world.

On August 11, 1993, 10 years to the day after the new company's

start, Terry announced his decision to step back from the day-to-day operations. With this decision, Garco's senior management team took the reigns. Ultimately, the five senior managers purchased the company from Terry, in 1996. It was at that time that Bill Savitz, only the third president in the company's 38-year history, ascended from within the organization.

Garco Building Systems is continuing its growth and performing better than at any time in its long history. What has driven this continued expansion and success is a passion that exists at all levels in the organization. As witnessed by the various independent certifications of quality and knowledge they possess, the people of Garco truly enjoy what they do and what they build. They take pride in being told time and again by their customers that they do it better than anyone else in their industry. The company's tagline, "Maximum Building Value," speaks to the culture of the service provided to their customers. In the measure of value which includes product quality and consistency, flexibility, engineering expertise and sophistication, high levels of customer service, and dependability, Garco Building Systems has proven its ability to perform.

Garco Construction

"Enjoy the journey" reads a sign in the lobby of Garco Construction's office on East Broadway in Spokane. Since its separation from Garco Building Systems in 1978, Garco Construction has indeed taken many wonderful journeys far-afield from its Spokane roots. With annual volume just over $1 million when acquired by Tim Welsh and Bob Carter in 1978, Garco Construction grew to over 50 times that size within its

Spokane Veterans Memorial Arena - Garco Construction, 1995. Photo by Explosive Illusions

first 20 years in business.

As a graduate civil engineer from the University of Washington, Welsh drove the company with his education and experience in and true passion for heavy industrial construction. With Kaiser Aluminum's two major facilities in Spokane, Garco was able to gain a foothold in the local industrial market. This experience acted as the means necessary to develop a name that could then be parlayed into other industrial client offices. The audiences gained included many regional companies within the mining industry, and led Garco to worksites all over the West, including Alaska.

As the resource-based construction industry waned in the late '80s and early '90s, Garco found it necessary to change course. In the early years, Garco performed work almost exclusively for private owners. With the change in economics, they purposely expanded into the public works arena. Less than 10 percent of Garco's work had been publicly funded in the past; by the late '90s, over 70 percent was publicly funded. This repre-

sented the best opportunity for growth for the company, allowing them to focus their efforts back home in Spokane.

Two years after the original purchase of the company in 1978, one of Welsh's best friends from childhood joined him as vice president of Garco. Frank Etter, who had been with Garco Building Systems for the previous eight years, brought a wealth of experience and energy to the company that helped motivate and drive them to growth. Also a graduate of the University of Washington, in personnel and industrial relations, Etter's attention to customer needs allowed the company to expand its expertise as an area leader in the design-

build method of project delivery. As a result, Garco's expanded staff of architects and engineers provided full turnkey design and general construction services for its expanded client base.

Garco Construction played a role in many of the major projects constructed in Spokane in the final quarter of the 20th century. Most notable of these is the Spokane Veterans Memorial Arena, which was the largest public works project ever awarded to a local contractor. The 12,500-seat arena is a major attraction landmark for the citizens of Spokane. Other notable projects are the 300,000 square-foot Spokane Valley Mall, Spokane's Waste to Energy Plant and the Airway Heights Prison. The 416-unit Wherry Housing Project, as well as the KC135 Hydrant Fueling facility, are two of the larger projects Garco Construction has undertaken at Fairchild Air Force Base.

Garco Building Systems and Garco Construction: two companies of common heritage. Although they were launched in different directions, their journeys remain remarkably intertwined in the fabric of Spokane.

Spokane Valley Mall - Garco Construction, 1997. Photo by Explosive Illusions

CAVANAUGHS HOSPITALITY CORPORATION

Cavanaughs Hospitality Corporation (CHC) has been serving the Northwest with superior products and services for over 60 years. The company owns, operates, acquires, develops, renovates, and repositions full-service hotels through its Cavanaughs Hotels division. Cavanaughs Hospitality Corporation also provides entertainment services, event ticketing, theatrical presentations, and other special events through its Cavanaughs Entertainment division. Property management services for third parties and the management of retail and office properties are offered through the Real Estate Services division of the company.

The predecessor to CHC, Goodale and Barbieri Companies, was founded in Spokane in 1937, by Lou Barbieri and Frank Goodale. The company focused its area of expertise on third party management services and real estate development in the city. In 1969, the company expanded its leadership in the community and added a residential division concentrated on affordable housing. The company's corporate offices continue to reside in Spokane where both family and business roots remain very strong.

In 1976, Goodale and Barbieri Companies founded a hospitality division, and developed their first hotel, Cavanaughs River Inn, located on the banks of the Spokane River. Over time, Goodale and Barbieri's service to the Northwest became so identified with the Cavanaughs Hotel brand that the company was renamed Cavanaughs Hospitality Corporation in 1998. That same year, the company began trading publicly on the New York Stock Exchange under the symbol "CVH." To date, Cavanaughs has grown its hotel division to 19 full-service hotels

located in Washington, Idaho, Montana, Oregon, and Utah.

Throughout the six decades Cavanaughs Hospitality Corporation has been in operation, the company philosophy has always remained the same. It is committed to providing and delivering high-quality products and services in each market served by CHC, with the greatest enthusiasm, integrity and respect. The company is committed to taking a leadership role within the communities it serves through active involvement in business, civic, charitable, trade and governmental organizations. It is also committed to hiring a staff of skilled, motivated and courteous associates, and to providing these associates with a safe and pleasant working environment that offers potential for accomplishment, self-fulfillment and growth.

Donald K. Barbieri is the chief executive officer and president of Cavanaughs Hospitality Corporation.

Don began working for his father Lou in 1969, and over the past 31 years has grown an exceptional company of over 2,500 associates who are committed to celebrating a spirit of genuine fun while serving their customers and each other.

As stated by Donald Barbieri, "Our company's legacy will be our reputation. Not how profitable we were, but did we produce great people, did those people deliver great service, and did they give training to others. The by-product of that will be financial success. We expect to continue to be a very profitable public company. Profit will be a by-product of growing a great company, growing a great group of associates, and growing a great workplace. That will be the legacy that will be known as Cavanaughs Hospitality Corporation."

Cavanaughs Hospitality Corporation is a leader in hospitality, entertainment and real estate services throughout the Northwest.

THE HEART INSTITUTE OF SPOKANE

Organizations come into existence because of individuals—often individuals committed to a cause. The Heart Institute of Spokane came to be because of physicians who pursued the cause of excellence.

In 1970, the National Institutes of Health held that heart attacks were caused by progressive atherosclerosis (thickening of the artery walls through the accumulation of fatty material) and that heart attacks are not reversible. Standard treatment was to "wait and see" before intervening. Spokane cardiologists and cardiac surgeons questioned this by observing that a heart attack indicates a serious dynamic problem in the heart muscle, one that requires immediate intervention. The cardiologists and cardiac surgeons established criteria and mechanisms to ensure that tests and surgery occurs within six hours after a heart attack. The results were astoundingly positive. Yet, national and international specialists considered Spokane full of "cowboys." The community's work was shunned, and for eight years this care—and criticism—continued.

Finally, inspired by observations of Spokane cardiologists, cardiac surgeons and nurse anesthetist Julie Spores, CRNA, Marcus DeWood, MD, researched and published dramatic findings: in every recorded heart attack, one of the arteries which surround and provide nutrients to the heart has been blocked by a blood clot. Immediate surgery restores blood supply to the heart. Spokane revolutionized the world's understanding of coronary events and changed how coronary medicine is practiced throughout the world. This renowned collective body of research became known as "the Spokane Experience."

Today The Heart Institute of Spokane, in operation since 1991, brings together leading cardiologists and cardiac surgeons sharing a vision of comprehensive cardiac care, prominent research and community education to promote healthier lifestyles.

The Heart Institute and its 50 member physicians serve a population of 1.4 million people within a 150-mile radius. It is the only freestanding outpatient heart catheterization facility in the Northwest.

Institute physicians run practices and collaborate through The Heart Institute. Institute member physicians regularly visit rural satellite offices in Washington, Idaho, Montana, and Oregon.

Research at The Heart Institute of Spokane is receiving national and international attention. Most importantly, the original and collaborative cardiovascular research projects are helping doctors and patients to better understand cardiovascular disease to the immediate betterment of human lives.

The Heart Institute's research has become nationally recognized. Established in 1991, The Institute serves 1.5 million people living within five states and Canada.

As a patient driven, hands-on center, The Heart Institute constantly seeks better answers to specialized problems. In this effort, The Institute collaborates with educators, other healthcare providers, government, corporations and the community, to create a world-class environment for the Inland Northwest in Spokane, in order to diminish the devastating effects of heart disease.

In these ways The Heart Institute of Spokane fulfills its mission, which is to reduce the impact of cardiovascular disease through: a) Cardiac care for patients—*applying the best* of what is known; b) Education for all—*sharing* what is known; c) Research for the medical community—*advancing beyond* what is known.

"Serving the Community, Contributing to the World."

HUMANIX PERSONNEL SERVICES

Julie Prafke went knocking on opportunity's door. She had worked in numerous companies in the Spokane and Coeur d'Alene areas, including state government, a securities business, a metal fabrication company and an insurance firm. Finally, while finishing her MBA in 1985, Prafke went to work for a national employment service and that door to opportunity opened wide. On July 26, 1986, she was able to open her own staffing service. Gail and Roger Smith provided financial support and backing. In its first year Humanix Personnel Services placed fewer than 600 temporary employees with total payroll of $225,000. By 1998, annual employee count had increased to 4004, with annual payroll exceeding $10,000,000.

In 1989 Julie purchased Humanix from the Smiths, through an Employee Stock Ownership Plan, which affords company ownership to all employees, full-time staff as well as temporary workers (those placed on assignment with other companies). Employees become participants through working a specified amount of time. No monetary contribution by employees is required. Each year the company is evaluated and stock is allocated to the employees' accounts based on their participation and the performance of the company.

The original office was located in a small office complex on the northside of Spokane. In 1991 an additional office was opened in Coeur d'Alene, Idaho; in 1994 another office was opened in the Spokane Valley. Over the years the company has expanded its facilities and now leases approximately 7,000 square-feet in each of its three locations.

By 1995 the company had recognized the importance of

Humanix Personnel Services staff, in August 1992, taken at "Red Flyer" at Riverfront Park in downtown Spokane.

providing computer skills to area employees. Humanix Learning Centers opened in Spokane in January 1996. "Our initial focus with the Learning Centers was not on the revenue, but on providing skilled workers to employers. Out of the businesses we surveyed during our program evaluation, 47 percent said skill levels were not where they needed them to be," said Julie Prafke. In late 1998 the Learning Centers began to offer computer certification courses in addition to the computer application classes.

Prafke says the success of Humanix can be attributed to the skilled, committed staff, several of whom have been with her since the beginning. She believes in empowering each staff member to "find a way to say 'yes.' It has been so rewarding watching people grow as the company has grown," says Prafke.

Humanix has a reputation for emphasizing the needs of all its employees. "That's why we

wanted the word "human" to be part of our company name." Testimony to this is the Family-Friendly Business Award Humanix won in 1998, one of many recognitions and awards the company and its employees have received. Staff members are encouraged to be active in community service; many serve with distinction on local councils and boards.

Prafke's axiom for growth and success is simple. She continually seeks to challenge herself and her staff to remain excited and engaged in their industry. Prafke's belief that successful entrepreneurship requires a people-oriented business attitude has paid off for her. "I was always taught that you should treat people the way you would like to be treated," Prafke says. "It's a pretty simple notion, really."

INLAND NORTHWEST DISTRIBUTING, INC.

Gary Verhey, founder and president of Inland Northwest Distributing, Inc., chose wisely when he named his fledgling corporation in 1972. Verhey's choice of the company's name was inspired by the geographical area called "The Inland Empire," the area reaching from the Cascade Mountains in Washington to the Rocky Mountains in Montana. He wanted to identify the new company with a description of its market area, and his inspiration later evolved into an official description of the market area defined by the former Inland Empire.

Inland Northwest Distributing, Inc., a wholesale distributor of floor covering and building specialties, started small—the total payroll in the first year of business amounted to less than $50,000 for five employees at the office and warehouse at 902 N. Dyer Rd. Since that time, the company has grown to include seven branches and 62 employees who service more than 2,000 accounts in central and eastern Washington, all of Idaho, all of Montana, northern Wyoming and the western Dakotas. The company, now located at N. 2003 Waterworks, supplies carpet, carpet cushion, vinyl flooring, ceramic tile, wood and laminate flooring, moldings, installation tools and other supplies to retail flooring specialty stores and installers.

Major product lines distributed by Inland Northwest Distributing include Mannington vinyl, wood and laminate flooring, American Olean ceramic tile and Johnsonite rubber flooring. Sixty-five percent of the company's sales are for residential applications; the remaining 35 percent are commercial flooring products installed in a wide variety of sites including Fred Meyer stores, Rosauers Supermarkets, the Spokane

Gary Verhey, founder and president.

Valley Mall, Shriners Hospital, the Land-Rover Auto showroom and area churches.

Characterizing the business as "a people business—the products come and go," Verhey credits the dedication of his employees and the development of strong customer relationships as crucial to the expansion of Inland Northwest Distributing. Several employees have devoted over 20 years to the company, and as a result are able to provide customers with well-informed and consistent service. "I believe in hiring good people and training them in our philosophy — to remember that our customers want to provide the best value to their customers."

Verhey, who majored in forestry at Duke University, spent five years with the U.S. Forest Service before joining the Roberts Company, originator of the tackless method of carpet installation, in Los Angeles in 1963.

During this time he established several independent distributors, including Anderson Supply in Spokane. After deciding to combine his love of the outdoors with his growing knowledge of the floor-covering business, Verhey moved his family to Spokane in 1969 and began the transition from Anderson Supply to Inland Northwest Distributing, Inc.

What began as a small corporation in 1972 has grown into a major business with annual sales of approximately six to eight million square-feet of floor coverings by sales representatives who travel more than 250-thousand miles each year. Verhey points to the continued consistency of "people, products and marketing programs" as the cornerstone of Inland Northwest Distributing Inc.'s success.

JENSEN DISTRIBUTION SERVICES

In 1883, the days when Eastern Washington was part of the vast western frontier, Jensen Distribution Services was founded by O.C. Jensen in Sprague territory of Washington.

Mr. Jensen belonged to the rank of adventurous pioneers who left native lands to seek fortune in the wide opportunities of America. He was born in Denmark, and as a young boy came to America, finding his way to California. From California he heard of the opportunities in the northwest and came to Sprague, which was one of the liveliest centers in this section of the country at that time.

His first partner Henry Brooke, later sold his interest to Charles King and operated under the name Jensen King & Company through 1895. In 1896, after a fire had destroyed most of the town of Sprague, the company merged with the firm Wolverton and Byrd, subsequently incorporated under the name Jensen-King-Byrd Company and relocated to Spokane. The company had its store in the Temple Court Building for several years until its expansion demanded additional space and it was moved to its present location at West 314-324 Riverside.

J. Scott and Alvin L. Jensen, sons of O.C., purchased Mr. King's interest in 1925, thereby changing the name of the corporation to Jensen-Byrd Co. O.C. continued as president of the company until 1928, the year of his death. The M. Seller Building, next to the W. 314 Riverside Building, was purchased in 1933. These facilities still serve as offices for the company. By the mid-1930s the Jensen family had purchased nearly all of the Byrds' interest.

To better serve its many

The first Jensen Store at 1883 Sprague.

customers, Jensen-Byrd's owners knew that additional warehouse space was needed. In 1935 a warehouse was added on International Way, followed soon by two more warehouses on the same street.

Distribution Services made a most significant expansive move in 1958 when the company acquired the wholesale operations of Marshall Wells Company, Spokane branch. At this time, merchandise was transferred from the three warehouses on International Way to the Marshall Wells warehouse at E. 131 Main, which was part of the acquisition.

In the early 1950s the company became a member of Liberty Distributors, a national group of aggressive and reputable hardware wholesale companies. As a result of this membership, Jensen Distribution Services had sub-licensed a group of independent hardware and home center dealers in Washington, Oregon, Idaho, Montana, Alaska and Nevada under a national association of Trustworthy Hardware dealers. At present, the company services over 180 of these Trustworthy Stores. J. Scott Jensen passed away in October 1981. Alvin L. Jensen passed away in October 1983 and his son, Stan A. Jensen is now chairman of the board. Stan A. Jensen's son Michael S. Jensen, is now president. In December 1981, the company made another major expansion when the inventory and certain assets were purchased from Pacific Marine Schwabacher, Seattle, Washington, the largest hardware wholesaler in the northwest and—founded in 1869—also one of the oldest. This was an important expansion, adding six states

Jensen Distribution Services today.

including Alaska and Hawaii to the area serviced. Additional warehousing was necessary, requiring two more in Spokane and a distribution center in Clearfield, Utah. Also in 1981, the company established a sales and promotion office in Seattle.

The company's commitment to the future continued in 1987 with the completion of a new 252,000 square-foot distribution center. This state-of-the-art facility sits on 30-acres west of Spokane, near Medical Lake.

In 1991, Liberty Distributors and Sentry Hardware merged and became Distribution America, North America's largest distribution network, with sales of over $2.5 billion. This enabled Jensen Distribution Services to carry the Trustworthy and Golden Rule Stores program. Jensen Distribution Services is currently an owner/member of D.A.

In January 1994 the company acquired the inventory for the independent hardware business from Morse Hardware in Bellingham, Washington, along with the Sentry Stores program.

On April 22, 1995 Jensen-Byrd Company became Jensen Distribution Services to demonstrate the changes that had occurred

within the organization over the past 112 years.

Today, Jensen Distribution Services employs over 250 people with 20 resident Territory Managers servicing over 220 program stores as well as home centers, independent hardware stores and mass merchants in 10 different states. An inventory of over 43,000 items allows for distribution of housewares, hand and power tools, plumbing, electrical, paint and paint sundries, sporting goods, lawn and garden, automotive, building supplies and farm supplies. The company currently services independent dealers and mass merchants in Alaska, California, Colorado, Idaho, Montana, Nevada, Oregon, Utah, Wyoming and Washington.

Four generations of the Jensen family have capably led this company into greater commitments with increased services to the retail stores and dedication to supplying its customers with the best service possible at the lowest costs. How does Jensen Distribution Services address the future? The company recognizes that it must be driven by sales and marketing and is taking steps to insure this mission is accomplished. Jensen's customers seek more services and support systems than ever before. Another area that is vital to the company's survival is technology. Jensen Distribution Services takes an active position to insure that technological advances are put to use within the organization.

Jensen Distribution Services is proud to have been part of Washington's history for the past 116 years, and looks forward to the opportunities and growth that the future holds.

INTEGRUS ARCHITECTURE

Bruce Walker began his architectural practice in 1953 in an abandoned elevator shaft of the elegant Davenport Hotel. In the early years, the firm had the good fortune to design a number of significant projects, the most notable being the headquarters office building for the Washington Water Power Company. This project, a joint venture between architects Bruce Walker and Ken Brooks, received a National Honor Award from the American Institute of Architects. It was an exciting project for Spokane, noted for its early use of curtainwall construction. In 1961, Walker now joined by John McGough was hired to design the Convent of the Holy Names. This very unique building was one of the last examples of the traditional convent.

Throughout the '60s, Walker & McGough's designs continued to shape the City of Spokane. The firm designed projects such as the Ridpath Motor Inn, Temple Beth Shalom, the U.S. Federal Building

Spokane Opera House, Convention Center, and Ag Trade Center, a legacy from the Expo '74 World's Fair and one of the most recognizable landmarks in Spokane.

Carnegie Library reborn as INTEGRUS Architecture offices. Principals include John Cuddy, Mark Dailey, Larry Hurlbert, William A. James, Gary Joralemon, George Nachtsheim, Arthur Nordling, John Plimley, Gordon Ruehl, Thomas Shine, and Gerald Winkler.

(a joint venture), St. Lukes Hospital, the Spokane County/City Public Safety Building, and the Farm Credit Banks Building.

The Expo '74 World's Fair brought a new excitement to the City of Spokane and to the now expanded firm of Walker McGough Foltz Lyerla. WMFL was selected to design the Washington State Expo Pavilion. Built on an old railroad site on the Spokane River, the building, now the Opera House and Convention Center, has become one of the most recognizable landmarks in Spokane.

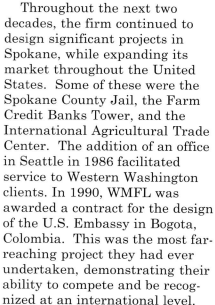

Throughout the next two decades, the firm continued to design significant projects in Spokane, while expanding its market throughout the United States. Some of these were the Spokane County Jail, the Farm Credit Banks Tower, and the International Agricultural Trade Center. The addition of an office in Seattle in 1986 facilitated service to Western Washington clients. In 1990, WMFL was awarded a contract for the design of the U.S. Embassy in Bogota, Colombia. This was the most far-reaching project they had ever undertaken, demonstrating their ability to compete and be recognized at an international level.

Looking to the future and recognizing the evolution of the new firm leadership, the name was changed to INTEGRUS Architecture in 1991. In 1992, the firm purchased the Carnegie Library located on the edge of Spokane's historic Browne's Addition for its new office. The old city library, which was built in 1904, had been abandoned for 12 years. The renovation design for the new office respected and enhanced its original architectural character. The building was placed on the National Register of Historic Places in 1993 and was presented an Historic Preservation Award that same year. This restored community treasure has been a catalyst for further development in its historic neighborhood.

INTEGRUS continues to shape the built environment of Spokane through its involvement on projects such as the Riverpoint Higher Education Campus, which includes the SIRTI Building, the Phase I Academic Building and the Health Sciences Building. The firm's award-winning designs are a lasting legacy to the City of Spokane.

LeMASTER & DANIELS PLLC

Ellis LeMaster was born in 1872 in Illinois. He began his accounting career by establishing an office in the Los Angeles Business College where he was introduced to his first and only formal training in accounting.

In 1901 Ellis became a traveling auditor for the Phelps Dodge Mining Company before accepting a part-time auditor's position for the growing city of Spokane Falls in 1905. The part-time position allowed him to start a part-time public accounting practice on the side.

Emery Clair Daniels.

By 1908 Ellis entered into partnership with Thomas C. Cannon, a chartered accountant from Canada. Spokane was growing rapidly because of the mining boom in northern Idaho, and Ellis' experience with Phelps Dodge was a helpful introduction to the mining community in both Idaho and Washington. He obtained many clients that formed the backbone of the firm. Ellis, and later his son Eustace, developed national reputations in the field of accounting for nonferrous mining. When Ellis became increasingly debilitated by asthma, Eustace joined the firm and quickly assumed his father's place in professional and civic arenas.

Mr. Cannon was an outstanding technician, but Ellis was the primary rainmaker. His friendly manner and many contacts in the mining and business community allowed LeMaster & Cannon to prosper. Many of the first contacts with timber companies, lumber mills, and banks began at this time, and Ellis established several memberships in civic organizations that would continue to be a tradition for the firm. He was a founding member of the downtown Spokane Rotary Club, a founder of the Spokane post of the American Legion, and served as treasurer of the Spokane Area Chamber of Commerce.

Emery Clair Daniels was born on February 14, 1892, in the Palouse. Clair graduated at the top of his high school class in 1910 and attended Kinman Business University for his formal training in accounting.

He went into partnership with Seth W. Crabtree and established the firm of Crabtree & Daniels in downtown Spokane. Clair was elected the first president of the new Spokane Chapter of the Washington Society of Certified Public Accountants. When Seth Crabtree died suddenly in 1922, Clair Daniels continued the practice, moving to the Symons Block next door to LeMaster & Cannon. The neighbor firms consolidated in 1926 to create LeMaster, Cannon & Daniels.

The dramatic closure of the nation's banks by President Roosevelt in 1933 opened the door for new opportunities for the firm. Banks were required to have a Statement of Solvency signed by a CPA before reopening. Clair seized this opportunity to travel to the rural areas and assist local banks with their Statement. This began the lifelong association with small eastern Washington communities

that would contribute over 60 percent of the firm's revenues and transform LeMaster & Daniels into one of the largest regional accounting firms in the nation.

In late 1936 Thomas Cannon suffered a fatal stroke and in January 1937 Ellis LeMaster was stricken by a heart attack and died at his desk. Shortly after the loss of the two founding members, the name was changed to LeMaster & Daniels and continued to prosper under the direction of Eustace LeMaster and E. Clair Daniels.

In 1957 Clair Daniels retired to Arizona until his death in 1980.

Ellis LeMaster.

Eustace LeMaster left the partnership in 1961 and died in 1964.

With the passing of these two great men, a page in history was turned, but the legacy they helped to create continued to grow. In 1960 a Colfax office was opened, followed by ones in Moses Lake, Othello, and Quincy. By the end of the 1990s, offices were opened in Omak, the Tri-Cities, Yakima, Spokane Valley, Grandview, Pullman, and Coeur d' Alene, Idaho. As the 21st century approaches, LeMaster & Daniels has grown to become one of the 40 largest accounting firms in the United States with offices in 12 locations and a staff of over 250.

LOOMIS, FARGO & CO.

From his youth to his later days as founder of the Loomis Armored Car Service Company, Lee B. Loomis was a true American pioneer. Throughout his life he consistently sought opportunity. Despite risks and uncertainty, his courage and persistence moved him to face the frontiers of his day.

Lee B. Loomis was born on June 24, 1870 in Elm Hall, Michigan. At the age of 10 his family moved to the Dakota Territory where he helped his father, George H. Loomis run a general store in the prairie. In his teens, he rode the range at his father's ranch in Ipswich, Dakota Territory. The Loomis family was caught up in the Indian uprising of 1883 and 1884, which included the Custer Massacre. In 1890, at the age of 20, Lee married, and in the same year was present at the last Sioux uprising, the Battle at Wounded Knee.

Lee tended stock until 1894, when he began a long trek to Seattle, Washington with his brother-in-law Charlie Jones. First, he sent his wife and three children ahead of him by paying their fares with $50 he borrowed. Then, he headed west and earned

Founder, Lee B. Loomis.

travel money in small towns along the way. In Bozeman, Montana he punched cattle and broke horses. In Missoula, Montana and Spokane, Washington he made money at numerous odd jobs. He sent most of his earnings to his wife in Seattle while building up a reserve for when they would reunite later that year.

During his first few years in Seattle, he operated a stock seed business. In 1896, he staked a claim on the old channel of Canyon Creek in Whatcom County, Washington. After just three trips earned him about $10 a day in gold dust, the pioneer spirit gripped him once again.

On July 24, 1897 Lee B. Loomis left for Alaska aboard the S.S. Mexico, the second ship to leave Seattle for the Klondike gold rush. The 900-mile passage brought Lee and hundreds of others to Dyea, Alaska. From here, he and his partner, Billy Hensell packed over grueling Chilkoot Pass to Lake Bennett. It was here that all of their supplies and the boat they had just purchased was stolen. Stranded without supplies or funds, Lee hiked back down to

Skagway where he spent the winter as a boat builder and packer.

Charlie Jones rejoined Lee in Skagway in the spring of 1898. They went to Dawson City, Yukon Territory and operated a general store as partners for the next five years. In 1903, Lee suddenly left for Nome in remote northwest Alaska. Stories of gold strikes, true or not, aroused his interest. Panning for gold with great optimism, he instead went $4,000 into debt. He then borrowed another $5,000 when he had the chance to purchase used outfits and provisions from men who gave up on the gold rush to return to the States. He resold the goods to incoming prospectors at a 100 percent profit. The next year Lee moved to Fairbanks, where rich gold strikes were also making headlines. With his earnings from these gold fields and other odd jobs, he got himself completely out of debt. He now owned four saddle horses, a one-half interest in a pack train of 10 mules and a one-third interest in a store.

In 1905 he started the Cleary Creek Commercial Company near Fairbanks. Known there as the "Four C's," they established the first free delivery on Cleary Creek, 30 miles north of Fairbanks. Their main business became dog sled transport service to nearby mines, carrying supplies directly to customers. Because of his personal integrity and reliability, Lee's business flourished. By request, he was then entrusted to guard and transport gold safely back to Fairbanks on behalf of his customers. It would be another 20 years until he started a similar service in the city with armored cars.

In 1906 Lee returned to Seattle, where he earned a living shipping horses to Alaska. Two years later he got a job in charge of the "Julia

Lee B. Loomis (fourth from left), son Walter (second from right), remainder of his family and his partner in front of the cabin he built in Fairbanks, Alaska, circa 1904.

B.," a Yukon River boat. He left Seattle pulling two barges destined for St. Michael, Alaska. During the two-month trip to the Yukon River he lost one of the barges in the ocean, due to stormy seas.

After that experience, Lee then spent the next 14 years in Seattle, where he owned Westlake Sales and Livery Stables. He was the main supplier of horses sold and shipped to Alaska. He also furnished horses for the city of Seattle, Seattle Fire Department, department stores, commercial houses and the U.S. Army at Fort Lewis. Following the death of his first wife in Seattle in 1920, he returned to Alaska.

In 1922 Lee took a position with the Northern Commercial Company in the Kuskokwim district. He headed two trading posts, Tokotna and McGrath on the Kuskokwim River. It was here that he shipped out 600-tons of goods annually,

Walter F. Loomis and Armored Car No. 1 and Charles W. Loomis next to Armored Car No. 225 off the assembly line in 1965.

which he traded to trappers for their furs and to miners for their gold dust at $16 an ounce.

In 1923, as postmaster in the Kuskokwim country, Lee hired Grace A. Anderson as clerk. She became his second wife, and has the added distinction of handling the first airmail ever received or dispatched in Alaska.

The first Loomis armored car, September 10, 1925. Lee B. Loomis is at left.

Lee bid farewell to Alaska in 1925 to settle down in Portland, Oregon. He took his entire $8,000 savings and commissioned a Portland carriage works to build an armored body on a new White truck chassis. The first armored

car west of St. Louis, it was put into service in Portland on September 10, 1925. His first customer was the Federal Reserve Bank, followed by several area banks. Businesses showed little interest in the armored car until a violent crime wave hit Portland in the late 1920s. A well-publicized robbery of the city's biggest department store was the turning point. They signed up, followed by the theaters, newspapers, mercantile firms, electric, steamship, motor and railway companies.

After his startup of this new industry proved successful, sons Walter and Leon assisted him with rapid expansion of the armored car operation. Walter headed startups in Vancouver, Canada in 1931, Seattle in 1932, Tacoma in 1935 and Spokane in 1936. Leon headed to California to open branches in San Francisco, Oakland and Sacramento in the early 1940s. Grandson Charles was taken under their wing and groomed for eventual control of the company.

Lee B. Loomis never lost interest in the affairs of Alaska. He

Loomis, Fargo and Co. truck No. 2122 servicing customers today.

The Loomis Dispatch

VOLUME XIII   NOVEMBER, 1960   NO. 11

Charles W. Loomis Assumes Company Presidency

WALTER F. LOOMIS yesterday announced important changes in the Company management structure.

By action of the Board of Directors, Walter F. Loomis was advanced to Chairman of the Board and Chief Executive Officer. Charles W. Loomis was advanced from Vice President-General Manager to President and General Manager. Glenn W. Whiteman, previously Treasurer, was made Secretary-Treasurer of the Corporation.

During the years of Walter's presidency, great strides were made in the Company's growth, adding five new branches and hundreds of new customers to the rolls.

Walter joined forces with his Father in the business in 1931 and after Lee B. Loomis' death in 1949 assumed the presidency. During recent years, he has devoted a great deal of his time toward the expansion of the Company, which has involved much traveling.

"Our continuous growth and development has clearly indicated the advisability of expanding our top management strength. It is our responsibility to our thousands of customers to maintain the strongest possible organization in every segment of the Company operations," Walter Loomis stated.

GLENN W. WHITEMAN joined the Company in 1945 after having completed his tour of duty with the Navy in World War II. Glenn has held the position of Treasurer of the Company since 1949.

CHARLES W. LOOMIS assumes the presidency after having served in all major departments. He joined the Company in 1946 and at once became a member of the operating staff of the Seattle Branch.

During the years that he wore the Loomis uniform, he became familiar with all the trials and satisfactions of custodians and drivers in their daily contacts with the customers. His next assignment was in the Accounting Department under Glenn Whiteman, Treasurer. From this he became involved in Branch management. This started a long period of traveling to our Branch cities and meeting the managers and operating personnel. The traveling has been going on ever since, though not as much lately as he has wished. His responsibilities as Vice President and General Manager have tended to keep him essentially in the Home Office. Few Loomis executives have a wider friendship among our operating crews and other personnel than does "Chuck".

Charles was born in Seattle. He attended Lincoln High School and became a graduate of Washington State College (University) in 1946.

During the War years, he was a Staff Sergeant in the Air Force, making 32 missions over Western Europe in a Boeing B-17. His family consists of Wife Betty, Cathy 13, Ann 11, and Walt 9.

It is the sheerest coincidence, but whether Dick or Jack is elected President on the second Tuesday in November, 1960, Charles will always remember the first Tuesday when his term as President began.

served as president of the Oregon-Alaska-Yukon Society, president of the International Sourdough Reunion and was chairman of the international convention of the Alaska-Yukon Society. His name was prominent in connection with presidential appointments to the Alaska International Highway Commission, created to administrate the construction of the

Alaska Highway. In regard to the nominations, an editorial in a Northwest newspaper wrote, "Loomis is a practical, hard-headed business man of good judgment who is in the transportation business and is thoroughly familiar with northern conditions. He is well known and trusted in Canada—a thoroughly good man for the position."

Revered by all of the newcomers to the industry, Lee was elected president-emeritus of the National Armored Car Association. Soon after, he passed away on April 1, 1949 at the age of 78.

Walter Loomis immediately succeeded his father as president of the company. For the next 11 years Walter guided its continual growth and profitability. In 1960, grandson Charles became president. Loomis Armored Car Service became a prominent national company under continuous family leadership for its first five decades.

The Loomis, Fargo & Co. of today maintains the same status as the premier service provider in the armored car industry. It is now the largest provider of armored car, automated teller machine and cash management services in the nation. The future looks bright as the company continues to pioneer better ways to serve its customers, just as Lee Loomis did.

Loomis, Fargo & Co. fully embraces the proud heritage of the Loomis name - the rugged tradition of Lee Loomis' first dog sled carrying miners' gold safely out of the wilderness, to his vision in 1925 of a fleet of modern armored cars.

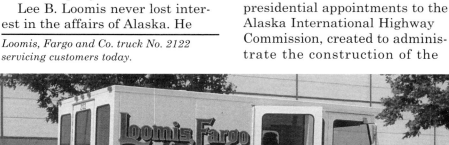

METROPOLITAN MORTGAGE & SECURITIES CO., INC.

Metropolitan Mortgage & Securities Co., Inc. was founded in Spokane in 1953 by C. Paul Sandifur and his brother Charles Sandifur. The Sandifur brothers had come to Spokane during the depression and had been engaged in the automobile business prior to founding Metropolitan. Paul Sandifur describes the history of the company in his book, *Just Give Me Real Estate*, which he wrote in his 88th year.

Metropolitan's original business was the buying of real estate contracts at a discount. Metropolitan raised money to do this by selling debenture bonds to the public and later by selling insurance products. Although the company was founded in Spokane, it soon opened offices in Alaska, Hawaii, and Tacoma, Washington.

Metropolitan Financial Center, 1999.

In the 1980s the company continued to open offices throughout the United States until it covered every part of the country. In the mid-1990s it moved most of its offices back to Spokane to take advantage of electronic communication and lower operating costs.

Metropolitan entered several businesses over the years including real estate development, the origination of mortgages, commercial lending, and life and casualty insurance. It also entered more esoteric businesses—some of which it later closed—such as mobile home sales, timeshare sales, campgrounds, and insurance brokerage.

In 1979 it set up a securities broker dealers and registered with the Securities and Exchange Commission. In 1981 it reached $100 million in assets. In 1988 Metropolitan renovated and opened a performing arts center "The Met," which it still runs and subsidizes.

In 1990 it reached $1 billion in assets. In 1995 it did the first securitization of seller financed real estate paper in Wall Street's history. Later it securitized timeshare paper and structured settlements.

In 1995 C. Paul Sandifur and his wife J. Evelyn Sandifur were tragically killed in an automobile accident. At that time, Metropolitan was the leading purchaser of real estate contracts and other seller financed debt in the United States. It was also a leading purchaser of lottery winnings, structured settlements, and other types of cash flows. In 1999 Metropolitan opened a leasing division.

C. Paul Sandifur, Sr., 1903-1995

Metropolitan and other companies owned by the Sandifur family have over $1.5 billion in total assets. The group has three life insurance companies and several other subsidiaries. It specializes in purchasing real estate contracts, mortgages, and other types of cash flows that are out of the main financial markets.

Metropolitan has been active in Spokane and the surrounding region. It is involved in several real estate projects and has aided in the development of high-tech business associations. It has a community affairs division that invests in community activities and self-help groups. It tries to minimize red tape in these efforts and help groups that otherwise would have difficulty getting funding.

In 1998 the company purchased a new headquarters building and participated in a major team-building process in preparation for the move. They called this "the Quantum Leap," and it involved the participation of virtually every employee of the company. Metropolitan believes it is well prepared to enter the new millenium.

MCVAY BROTHERS, INC.

Over one hundred years ago in 1883, a young boy made the journey overland from Kansas to the Spokane area. Little William Harrison McVay had just lost both of his parents to an influenza epidemic that had swept his hometown. A neighbor family, the Salmons, were kind enough to take him in. William grew up in the Spokane area, became a postman, and married Mary Elizabeth Carder. They had seven children: Julian, Harrison, Addison, Ken, William, Warren, and Aubrey. Unfortunately, Aubrey died in a tragic house fire.

The family eventually moved to the Mead area, where the boys comprised a significant percentage of the small school's population. Harrison, better known as Harry, graduated a year early to ensure that Mead would have a record graduating class—in the neighborhood of 20 students.

In 1933, William, the father, died suddenly. This left the family

Spokane Valley Roofing & Insulation in 1946.

McVay Brothers' 3106 N. Argon location in 1958.

nearly destitute. The boys were forced to work at an early age. After doing a few odd jobs, Julian, who was called JD by everyone familiar with him, opened up a small roofing business. It was located in the Hutton Building.

Harry joined the company in the late 1930s. Times were tough, and sacrifices had to be made. Warren was forced to give up his dream of going to college. He and Addison joined the company in the early '40s. The hard work did have its triumphs as the boys made enough money to send Ken to Whitworth College. He went on to

become a Seventh-day Adventist minister.

After military stints in the war, the boys went back to work. They moved to an office on East Trent Avenue, just outside of Millwood. Spokane Valley Insulation and Roofing operated until JD retired in 1955. He moved to Loon Lake, where his son eventually ran McVay Realtors. Harry and Warren changed the company's name to McVay Brothers.

In 1958 they moved to the former Potlatch Lumber yard in Millwood. The company still operates its retail and siding wholesale operations at this location. Harry and Warren worked long hours to turn McVay Brothers into a successful venture.

During the '50s and '60s, Harry and Warren McVay spent most Mondays through Thursdays canvassing out-of-town customers. A typical day began at 8:00 am with four men known as canvassers going door-to-door or farm-to-farm soliciting business. Harry and Warren were the "closers" who would then attempt to sell a siding or roofing job if there was any interest. The men usually worked late, often not finishing until after 10:00 pm. Fridays were reserved for scheduling and other business.

The fast pace had its human side, too. Harry found time to serve briefly as a trustee for Whitworth College and as president of the Union Gospel Mission. The brothers thought nothing of accepting IOU's from customers who had fallen on hard times. They rarely charged customers for small repairs, knowing that when the time came, they would be remembered.

Harrison McVay, Jr. joined the company in 1967. As a former CPA, he brought new controls to the company. Running the

Harry and Warren McVay in the early '70s.

day-to-day operations of the firm, he allowed Harry and Warren to focus their attention on sales. The company expanded rapidly.

In the 1970s McVay Brothers became the first siding company in Spokane to advertise on television. Early adds featured Harry's daughter Becky as the spokesperson for the company. Today, countless customers still ask about her.

Harry and Warren retired by the early 1980s, leaving Harrison, Harry's son, as the president. He ceased roofing operations in 1983 to focus on siding and windows. It turned out to be a wise choice. In 1990, Harrison introduced seam-less steel siding to the Inland Northwest. It remains the mainstay of the company's siding business today. He also began the company's wholesale siding business in 1979.

Mark and Mike McVay, the third generation of the McVay family involved in the business, went to work for McVay Brothers

Bus advertising in 1964.

in 1990 after stints at Whitworth College and Washington State, respectively.

In 1993 the new Brothers and Harrison purchased a window manufacturing company. After some early difficulty, the window plant (as it is known) has grown to occupy a 30,000 square-foot building on East Trent, not far from the old Spokane Valley Insulation and Roofing Building.

The plant manufactures a complete line of both vinyl and composite windows. McVay Brothers Composite Windows are made from ABS and ASA plastics. This allows the products to be made in darker colors than typically found with vinyl windows. The retail/wholesale location sells and installs several varieties of siding and window products.

Harrison retired in early 1999, leaving Mark McVay as president and Mike McVay as vice-president of sales and marketing.

Throughout the '90s the company has been a mainstay on the *Qualified Remodeled* Top 500 list, a compilation of the top remodels in the country. McVay Brothers has also appeared on *Remodeling Magazine's* Big 1000 list. In addition, the company has been nominated for the Spokane Chamber of Commerce Agora Award twice.

Today, the company ships and installs siding and window products all over the Northwest and beyond. Siding has been sent as far as Russia, while a small orphanage in Romania has a little piece of Spokane in its McVay Windows. McVay Brothers also employs nearly 150 Inland Northwest residents in its two facilities. Mark McVay, the company's president attributes their success to the "numerous dedicated employees and family members who will go to any length to satisfy our customers."

PAINE, HAMBLEN, COFFIN, BROOKE & MILLER LLP

A merging of discovery, excitement and intensity set the tone for the development of the Paine Hamblen Law Firm.

The discovery of electric power in the Spokane River nearly coincided with the first partnership of firm lawyers, for it was in June 1893 that Frank T. Post resigned his position as corporation counsel for the City of Spokane and joined Judge Richard B. Blake to form a law partnership. Shortly thereafter, Frank Post became general counsel for an emerging company that drew its strength from the Spokane Falls, Washington Water Power Company, now Avista Corporation.

Later, when Frank Post became president of Washington Water Power Company (1930-1939), Spokane native Alan G. Paine (1895-1958) became a partner in the newly-named firm of Post, Russell, Davis and Paine.

Later generations of Paine Hamblen attorneys continued to carry on a tradition of integrity, professionalism and community service. The modern firm dates

Shaun M. Cross, managing partner since 1997.

Herb Hamblen in a rowboat. Herbert M. Hamblen, chair of the Spokane Parks and Recreation Foundation, 1959 to 1986.

back to June 1, 1980, when Paine, Lowe, Coffin, Herman & O'Kelley merged with another of Spokane's oldest firms, Hamblen, Gilbert & Brooke.

Thus, the names "Paine" and "Hamblen" emerged as icons of powerful "voices" rising above the water rolling over Spokane Falls. This, of course, enhanced the stature of other leaders of the firm, including Phil Brooke, Sr. (1892-1991), Roy Lowe (1888-1972) and Harold Coffin (1908-1995.) Fittingly, the civic leadership of early partners has become memorialized in the names of many places in the city of Spokane: Post Street (Frank Post), Hamblen Park and Hamblen Elementary School (Laurence Hamblen), and the Herbert M. Hamblen Conservation Area.

The excitement of the second-generation Paine Hamblen lawyer, Herbert M. Hamblen (1905-1994), clearly expresses the underlying foundation of the firm's continuing long-term client-attorney relationships. He captured this joyful intensity in a speech in which he reminisced about his childhood trip in 1912 to Blacktail Beach on the shores of Lake Pend Oreille. He recollected having discovered flat skipping stones and spawning masses of black fish with red and yellow stripes. In nature, he said, he discovered "excitement, happiness and wonder beyond anything I had imagined."

Likewise, as "one tough advocate," Herb Hamblen brought this same joyful intensity to his practice of law and civic service. He not only rose to become the Speaker of the Washington House of Representatives from 1947 to 1948, but he also followed in his father's footsteps by serving for 27 years as the chair of the Spokane Parks and Recreation Foundation from 1959 to 1986. Phil Brooke, Jr. (a contemporary and second-generation partner) later eulogized Herb Hamblen by simply observing that, "he liked what he did and he was good at it."

Paine Hamblen's tradition of strength and success continued to attract new combinations of lawyers. In 1985 Paine Hamblen merged with a Coeur d'Alene, Idaho law firm founded by one of Idaho's foremost attorneys, Eugene L. Miller. With the firm's most recent merger in 1999, the Spokane law firm of Chase Hayes Kalamon rounded out Paine Hamblen's expanding commitment to the field of labor and employment and to the healthcare industry of the region.

Today a similar sense of discovery, excitement and intensity lays the foundation for long-term relationships with over 200 major clients in the Inland Northwest, including Avista Corporation,

Sacred Heart Medical Center, Telect, Inc., PEMCO Insurance Companies, City of Spokane, Burlington Northern Santa Fe Railroad Co., Pathology Associates Medical Laboratories, Hecla Mining Company, Mutual of Enumclaw Ins. Co., Whitworth College, Providence Services, Washington Trust Bank and Inland Northwest Bank.   Paine Hamblen has grown from the first two partners of Post and Blake to a total of 190 employees, including over 70 attorneys. Practice groups have been developed in fields most useful to the business community, such as commercial; healthcare;

tax; estate planning; labor and employment; litigation; bankruptcy; corporate; transactional; securities; real estate; environmental and insurance defense law.

Building on over 100 years of growth, Paine Hamblen is now the largest independent law firm between Seattle and Minneapolis. And the joyous, intense "voices" of the past continue to resonate in the leadership of Paine Hamblen. Shaun M. Cross, the present managing partner, envisions a growing, dynamic full-service law firm that will meet the needs of the Spokane-area's complex business community. Today, the

Post Street, circa 1909 (named after founder Frank T. Post) looking north toward the Spokane River from just south of First Avenue. The Washington Trust Financial Center in which Paine Hamblen's present offices are located replaced "Graham's" paper store and the "Bandbox" theater between the Pacific Hotel, seen on the right of the photograph, and the larger building right-center, the Peyton Building.

view down Post Street looking toward the Spokane River includes the offices of Paine Hamblen in the midst of a busy, exciting and intense community.

165

POTLATCH CORPORATION

Potlatch Corporation originated in 1903, just a few miles from Spokane, in North Central Idaho. It was founded by a group of lumbermen that included Frederick Weyerhaeuser. The company's first sawmill was built in 1904-05 near the site of an early "potlatch," a Native American celebration of gift giving and good will. The mill and the town constructed for its workers were named for the celebration.

The Depression forced the 1931 merger of three Idaho companies in which Frederick Weyerhaeuser had interests: Potlatch Lumber Co., Edward Rutledge Timber Co. in Coeur d'Alene and Clearwater Timber Co. in Lewiston. The resulting company—Potlatch Forests, Inc.— continued to expand in Idaho and Washington.

Expansion and acquisition: Potlatch acquired Southern Lumber Co. of Warren, Arkansas in 1956 and four more companies in southeastern Arkansas in later years. The company built a pulp and paperboard mill at Lewiston in 1950 and later acquired a fine printing paper operation in Pomona, California. In 1963, pulp from the Lewiston operation also made possible the construction of a tissue mill to produce private label tissue products. In 1977, Potlatch constructed a modern bleached pulp and paperboard operation at Cypress Bend, Arkansas, near the town of McGehee.

Coated Fine Papers: Potlatch expanded its fine printing papers business by merging with Northwest Paper Co. in 1964. Founded in 1898, Northwest Paper operated mills in Cloquet and Brainerd, Minnesota, and had considerable timber holdings in the state.

Potlatch's corporate offices moved from Lewiston to San Francisco in the mid-1960s. The company expanded into packaging and real estate and acquired mills in South America and Western Samoa. During the 1970s and 1980s, the company sold many of these interests and concentrated on its core domestic businesses. In 1997, the corporate headquarters were moved to Spokane, Washington.

Better Utilization; modernized facilities: In the 1930s, Potlatch earned an early reputation for applied product research and progressive forest management. Potlatch built the nation's first Pres-To-Log operation, to make use of sawdust, at Lewiston. In the late 1940s, Potlatch built one of the region's first veneer and plywood operations at Lewiston. Potlatch acquired an Idaho plywood plant, at St. Maries, and built another at Pierce in the mid-1960s. Particleboard was added in the mid-1970s at Post Falls, Idaho. Company research led Potlatch to build the nation's first oriented strand board (OSB) plant in Minnesota in 1981. The company now operates three OSB plants in

Potlatch Lumber Co. and the town of Potlatch as they appeared c. 1920. Founded in 1903 as Potlatch Lumber Co. and later becoming Potlatch Corporation, the company moved its headquarters to Spokane in 1997.

Minnesota, at Bemidji, Cook and Grand Rapids.

In 1993, Potlatch constructed a new tissue-converting complex in North Las Vegas, Nevada, to more efficiently serve the southwestern market for private label tissue products.

Potlatch Today: Potlatch has completed a 15-year, multi-billion dollar modernization program. The company currently has more than 20 manufacturing sites and 1.5 million-acres of timberland in Idaho, Minnesota and Arkansas, and also operates a 22,000-acre hybrid poplar plantation in northeastern Oregon. Sales in 1998 were $1.6 billion. The company is listed on the New York Stock Exchange with the trading symbol PCH.

ROCKWOOD CLINIC, P.S.

The Rockwood Clinic name has been recognized in the Inland Northwest since the 1930s. The Clinic derives its name from the district known as Rockwood on the South Hill of Spokane. The first "Rockwood Clinic Hospital" opened its doors to 10 patients with a staff of four in 1930. The founder was Dr. William W. Robinson. Dr. Robinson grew up in Spokane and attended Rush Medical College in Chicago before returning to Spokane to establish his practice. At the time, Dr. Robinson was quoted as saying, "The hospital will be giving a new type of service where a complete examination and necessary medical and surgical services will be available under one roof under the close personal supervision of the physician in charge."

Dr. Robinson's practice did not begin without some controversy. He started the hospital after he was shunned by the medical community for testifying against a colleague in a malpractice lawsuit. While widely accepted and supported by his patients, Dr. Robinson realized it would be impractical to practice by himself, and enlisted an old friend, Dr. Harold Pederson to join him. It was quite a few

The present-day Rockwood Clinic, built in 1987.

years before Dr. Pederson and any of the other physicians who followed him were accepted in the medical community in Spokane, due to their association with Dr. Robinson.

However, the practice prospered until the majority of its physicians were drafted or enlisted at the start of World War II, necessitating the closing and sale of the hospital building to Sacred Heart Hospital. The "Rockwood Clinic" reopened in 1945 when Dr. Robinson returned to Spokane and began recruiting his colleagues to join him in a new style of medicine, the "group practice," or Mayo Clinic model. Its purpose was "to employ duly-licensed physicians, nurses and other assistants to furnish such medical and surgical treatments as patients might require."

In 1957, the Clinic moved to a larger facility on Eighth Avenue just west of Sacred Heart. Due to the rapid growth in Spokane's medical economy, physicians were added yearly from the 1960s to the 1980s. Planning for a new building to accommodate additional specialties began in 1984, and culminated with a grand opening of a 103,000 square-foot facility on East Fifth Avenue in the fall of 1987. This new building included

Capt. Wm. W. Robinson, WW II

the added specialties of primary care—family practice, pediatrics and obstetrics/gynecology—plus an urgent care center. The present clinic also serves as the center of the Rockwood Clinic satellite system that provides primary care services throughout the greater Spokane area.

During the past decade Rockwood Clinic has established a research department and Medical Research Foundation to allow physicians to participate in research and development of new pharmaceutical diagnostic therapies.

Today, the Rockwood Clinic continues in the spirit of Dr. Robinson while expanding its mission of serving the people of the Inland Northwest. Twenty-six medical specialties and over 100 physicians and 600 staff members work in nine facilities located throughout Spokane County. The Clinic continues to be owned and governed by its physicians, who believe that the group practice model emphasizes an integrated patient-focused approach to medicine and a commitment to working together in the "tradition of caring" that has become Rockwood Clinic's hallmark for over 70 years.

SACRED HEART MEDICAL CENTER

Healing requires both faith and science. This is the guiding conviction behind Sacred Heart Medical Center, which traces its beginnings to 1886 and the charitable mission of the French-Canadian Sisters of Providence.

As the new millennium dawned, Sacred Heart reaffirmed this link of spirit and body in a range of facilities for everyone in Spokane, its impact far greater than is measurable in dollars, beds and staff.

The Sisters of Providence was founded as the Filles de Charité, Servantes des Pauvres (Daughters of Charity, Servants of the Poor) in Montreal in 1843. Thirteen years later, Sister Joseph of the Sacred Heart led five Sisters to the Pacific Northwest in answer to a call from the Bishop of Nisqually. Starting in Fort Vancouver, Washington, they worked as caregivers and began establishing schools and hospitals throughout the area, eventually numbering more than two dozen.

In 1886, Mother Joseph and Sister Joseph Arimathea arrived in Spokane. They built the hospital on a two-block lot at the corner of Front Street (now Spokane Falls Boulevard) and Browne. Ground breaking took place on July 2, the feast of the Sacred Heart, giving the hospital its name. Mother Joseph served as architect and construction supervisor—and sometimes carpenter, building inspector, and fundraiser. In January 1887, Sacred Heart Hospital opened with 31-beds to serve the town's 3,000 people. In February, the county commissioners granted the Sisters a contract to care for the county's poor.

Sacred Heart grew with the community. In 1888, the hospital had a medical staff of six and added a wing, doubling its bed count to 62. Refusing to turn away

The original Sacred Heart Hospital, built by Mother Joseph at Front and Browne Streets in 1886. Photo is circa 1900 after two wings had been added to the original building.

anyone in need, the Sisters found places for as many as 130 patients the next autumn, when fever struck.

Spared during Spokane's great fire in 1889, the original hospital served the city as its population grew to 20,000 in 1890 and more than 100,000 in 1910. That year, the Sisters opened a new, 300-bed hospital, which contained a separate maternity facility. True to the order's mission, it also included a dining hall for the needy. The building was at the Medical Center's current location, Eighth Avenue and Browne.

The move was foreshadowed as early as 1892 when the Great Northern Railway bought right-of-way across part of the hospital's property. In 1902, Sacred Heart added a new wing, but continuing pressure for a larger facility, plus the increasing proximity of tracks, made moving to a new site inevitable. Construction, visualized as early as 1900 but postponed by shorter-term needs, began in 1907.

With the city needing increasingly sophisticated medical care, Sacred Heart Hospital contributed to professional training through its nursing school, internship program, and special technical schools.

It opened the School of Nursing in 1898 to provide trained personnel for a patient population grown too large for the Sisters to care for personally. It prepared nurses for medical service until the mid-1970s, when area hospitals abandoned in-house training programs in favor of university-trained nurses.

The hospital established medical internships to train physicians in 1931 and a School of Medical Technology in 1932. Its School of Anesthesia opened in 1937, formalizing training programs begun 20 years earlier.

Sacred Heart began organizing its functions into departments in the late 1910s. First was the radiology department, opened in 1919 in a corner of the surgery area. Then, and in the years that followed, Sacred Heart was a noted surgical center, attracting prominent physicians to observe operations.

The Department of Laboratory Medicine, also opened in 1919, over the next 40 years became a major medical resource for doctors and hospitals throughout the Inland Northwest.

The first open-heart surgery performed in Spokane was at Sacred

Heart in 1959 and it became home to the Inland Empire Artificial Kidney Center in 1963. Five years later, it pioneered in-home dialysis for kidney patients.

For all its prominence, however, Sacred Heart Hospital and the Sisters of Providence faced a difficult decision in the late 1960s. Its physical plant had become inadequate. The choice was to rebuild or to close. The order recognized that changes in governmental policies increasingly affected the way they could provide medical services. Some voices suggested they might serve the needy more directly without the administrative responsibilities of a major medical institution. After much deliberation, however, the Sisters concluded the hospital was essential.

The decision to borrow money for rebuilding took the Sisters of Providence, in the words of their administrator, Sister Peter Claver, "back to our historic commitment" to fill unmet needs, and to refuse no one, regardless of ability to pay.

Since the dedication in 1971 of the $35-million Sacred Heart Medical Center, few have doubted that the order made a wise decision. It has continued to provide leadership in the Spokane medical community and to reflect in its policies and priorities the original commitment of the Sisters of Providence: the Christian mission of caring for those in need.

In the early 1970s, Sacred Heart installed state-of-the-art diagnostic radiology equipment.

In 1976 it opened its Medical Outreach Clinic at the Spokane Catholic Diocese's House of Charity to attend to the needs of homeless men, women and children. It was the only free clinic of its kind in the area. By 1999, a volunteer team of physicians, backed by the hospital's emer-

Sacred Heart Medical Center in 1999.

gency department, was treating more than 2,200 people annually, for everything from high blood pressure to infectious diseases. In addition, each month Sacred Heart's Maternity Clinic provided hope and compassion to more than 200 pregnant women who might not otherwise have had access to prenatal care.

In 1984, Sacred Heart completed a new building that included 25 beds for physical therapy and rehabilitation, and 72 psychiatric beds, part of which was dedicated to child and adolescent mental health care.

Emphasizing the link between faith and science, Sacred Heart developed the Providence Center for Faith and Healing. In 1982, Sister Michelle Holland envisioned such a center. The building and its gardens opened in 1999 and were described by Center director Susan Keyes as a "healing haven and a place for prayer, growing, seeking and accepting."

In the 1990s, the Medical Center began working to bring education and early diagnosis of breast cancer to women throughout the Spokane area. This dream

began with Sister Ethel Richardson, part of Sacred Heart for more than 50 years and herself a victim of this disease. It was realized through the efforts of a team of women from Sacred Heart's Women's and Oncology Services, and Inland Imaging, LLC. A Mobile Mammography Coach went on the road in 1999, reaching women in outlying communities, at their workplaces and at community and retirement centers.

As the century ended, Sacred Heart Medical Center had more than 623 beds. Its equivalent of almost 4,000 full-time employees and well over 40,000 volunteer hours a year made it Spokane's second-largest private employer. Its staff was performing more than 24,000 surgeries, dispensing more than 2,400,000 prescriptions, treating more than 39,000 emergency patients, and delivering more than 2,000 babies each year.

Such statistics, however, barely begin to measure the importance to its community of Sacred Heart Medical Center's ministry and medical mission.

SPOKANE AIRWAYS

Only history buffs would know that the "Spokane Airways" name on the trucks that fuel airliners at Spokane International Airport salutes the earliest days of aviation here. In fact, the name is reminiscent of the roaring '20s, when flight captured the interest of early enthusiasts and entrepreneurs.

After World War I, the thrill of flight soared into the hearts of Spokane's visionaries who championed the growth of aviation. Seeing the tremendous possibilities an aviation industry would bring

Refueling of the "Tin Goose" at Felt Field—1928. Photo by Jim McGoldrick and Libby Photo

to the Inland Northwest, the early supporters actively pursued the development of a National Guard Squadron and Training Facility. These visionaries were successful.

The 116th Aviation Squadron base came to Spokane and the "National Guard Airfield" was built in a field between Parkwater and the river in the Spokane Valley. Once the airfield was in place, the stimulant for aeronautical development grew from the military budget.

Activity at the "field out by Parkwater"—later named after Buhl Felts, an early airman—captivated public interest. From that interest, entrepreneurs from

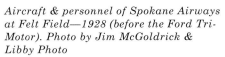

Aircraft & personnel of Spokane Airways at Felt Field—1928 (before the Ford Tri-Motor). Photo by Jim McGoldrick & Libby Photo

the booming lumber, mining and business sectors recognized that air transport would be a key factor in the development of Spokane as a regional service center. In order to expand that vision, the county acquired additional acreage adjacent to the National Guard Airfield in order to encourage development of aviation-oriented businesses.

Spokane Airways was among the first privately financed companies formed at Felts Field. By 1928, the company, run by Sam Wilson, a businessman involved in the mining industry, began providing aircraft maintenance, charter and refueling there. Spokane Airways also brought the first "modern passenger airliner," a Ford Tri-Motor, to the community. The "Tin Goose" as it was fondly called, carried 11 people plus crew at speeds of 110-miles per hour and was replete with stewardess and amenities for its passengers' comfort.

At this time, Nick Mamer, a Spokane aviation pioneer who found support and encouragement from local business leaders including Clarence "Cip" Paulsen, Louis Wasmer and others, was investi-

Spokane Airways Flight Center, 1999. Left to right: Richard Chastek, owner and president, his wife Margaret and sons Mark and John. Photo by Spokane Journal of Business

gating a northern route for flights between the northwest and the Twin Cities/Chicago area. Mamer saw the northern route as a way to open up commerce between the midwest and northwest. Mamer would become the regional manager of the fledgling Northwest Airways Co., which changed its name to Northwest Airlines, Inc. in 1934. By the mid-1930s, Northwest Airlines had developed the northern mail route that brought airmail into Spokane, and Mamer was the chief pilot on that route.

In the meantime, Mamer formed a partnership with Roy Schreck under the name Mamer-Schreck Air Transport Company, Inc. that provided him with a local tie. The Mamer-Schreck Air Transport Company, along with the Lamb, Wallace, Calkins and other schools trained hundreds of

pilots in the later half of the 1930s and throughout the war years.

It wasn't long before commercial and business aviation outgrew the airport by the river, and county commissioners once again began looking toward the future. To continue to stimulate aeronautical development in Spokane, prominent businessmen such as Vic Dessert, Joe Albi, Harlan Peyton, and W.H. Cowles argued for the relocation of a modern airfield. Thus, by the late 1930s the county commissioners purchased land "in the vicinity of Cheney Junction" for a "super airport" unofficially known as the Sunset Airport.

The Great Depression had left many men without work, and by 1939, the Works Progress Administration—a work program created by U.S. President Franklin D. Roosevelt that offered honest work to the unemployed—cleared and leveled the land for the new airport. However, with the rumors of war dancing in the wind, the Army Air

Force dismissed the WPA in 1940 and completed the project, naming the airport "Geiger Field."

Although the landing field had been completed, commercial development of the super airport was on hold until after the war when the U.S. Government ceded title to the city and county of Spokane.

With the Tri-Motors long gone and the frenzy of pilot training long past, the Mamer-Schreck Air Transport operations were combined with those if its sole shareholder, Spokane Airways.

Then, in 1964, as chair of the Aviation Committee of the Chamber of Commerce, Jim McGoldrick oversaw the commission of the new terminal on the northwest side of Geiger Field. The new terminal is now known as Spokane International Airport. Spokane Airways moved its operations into the airline facilities on the southeast side of Geiger Field.

In 1988 Spokane Airways was acquired by Richard Chastek. Chastek, who once watched the airplanes taking off and landing at Felts Field from a fence on his father's fur farm, returned to his fascination with aviation after a career in law and business.

Richard and Margaret Chastek and their two sons Mark and John, have significantly and successfully expanded the scope of their family-owned business. Spokane Airways now meets more than 80 passenger flights a day at the main airport terminal and more than 20 freight planes a day on the cargo ramp on the

west side of the airport.

On the east side of the airport, Spokane Airways' Flight Center provides services for base customers and itinerant business and private aircraft ranging from Piper cubs to Air Force One, 747s, Russian Antonovs and everything in between. The Flight Center greets prime ministers, presidents, movie greats, rock stars, business magnates, and moms and dads with kids and the family dog with equal courtesy.

Spokane Airways' Flight School has trained pilots that have joined the U.S. Marines, United States Air Force, and U.S. Navy, have found positions on the flight decks of Northwest Airlines, United Air Lines, Southwest Airlines, Horizon and Piedmont, have flown the bush routes of Alaska, pilot the plush cockpits of corporate jets, and fly small planes for the simple joy of flying.

Spokane Airways also has charter flights that transport passengers, mail and freight throughout the United States and Canada, daily. Its freight handling department has grown from a small forklift and a rental loader to three specialized aircraft container loaders capable of raising 15,000 pounds to a height of 15 feet in seconds. On a daily basis, the handlers load dozens of 6' high containers each carrying 3,000 to 5,000 pounds of mail and packages into the cavernous cargo holds of waiting jets. During the Christmas season, these numbers triple.

There has been a significant increase in handling and support of super jets as well as smaller regional cargo aircraft. Spokane Airways maintenance personnel provide maintenance and repair services for private and commercial airline ground equipment,

Cargo handling of mail & package by Spokane Airways at Spokane International Airport, 1999.

and the aircraft personnel provide maintenance and service for private and commercial aircraft throughout the region. Additionally, the maintenance department is on call 24-hours-a-day for any airlines' requirements.

Throughout the last 70 years, Spokane Airways has been service-oriented and growth-minded. Now, with the Chastek family at the helm, the company is indeed ready to step into the next millennium. Under the Chasteks' sound guidance, Spokane Airways will continue to meet the demands of a growing community and blend its honorable tradition of service, professionalism and vision.

JOHN STONE/JOHN STONE DEVELOPMENT, L.L.C.

John Stone was born in Great Falls, Montana in 1943. He moved with his family to Spokane when he was two years old, where he has remained a lifelong resident. John attended St. Aloysius grade school followed by Gonzaga Preparatory High School and graduated from Gonzaga University in 1966. Upon graduation John entered the emerging commercial computing field, ultimately teaching at North Idaho College and founding a computer services bureau.

Utilizing the profits from the bureau, John entered the fledgling mini-storage development business in 1973. Over the next 20 years, he built a total of 27 mini-storage facilities in Washington, Idaho and California, comprising over 460,000 square-feet. During this period, John also purchased, entitled and sold over multiple tracts of land throughout the West Coast.

In the late 1980s and early '90s, John Stone, along with his two sons Brad and Bryan, began expanding his company, through the addition of in-house construction managers and real estate specialists, and diversifying the focus of his developments to additional market segments. He first entered the luxury apartment market in Spokane and followed

AlderCrest Apartments, 47 apartment units on First Hill, Seattle, Washington built 1998/1999.

The Allegro, 141 apartment units, plus commercial University district, Seattle, Washington built 1998/1999.

by developing senior housing, including independent living, assisted living, and Alzheimer's facilities. His projects in Spokane have included the Indian Canyon Apartments, Stonecrest Apartments, Ridgestone Apartments and the Park Place Retirement Community in the Spokane Valley. He followed these projects with additional senior housing projects in Idaho, California and Nevada, including Forest Place Retirement Community in Coeur d'Alene, Idaho.

In the late 1990s, John Stone Development re-entered the Seattle market and quickly secured a name as one of the most active developers of mixed-use and residential projects in downtown Seattle, where they actively continue to develop. Projects in Seattle have included The Lenora in Belltown, The Allegro in the University District, the Aldercrest Apartments on First Hill, the Pete Gross House for the Fred Hutchinson Cancer Research Center in the Cascade District and the Admiral Heights Retirement

Community in West Seattle. In 1999 John Stone led the acquisition of a 74-acre parcel of land on Northwest Boulevard in Couer d'Alene, Idaho, which was formerly a lumber mill and includes over 3,500 acres of riverfront land on the Spokane River. Work is underway to complete a high-end commercial and residential development on the site, that will benefit the city of Coeur d'Alene. This large, in-city property is considered to be part of the gateway to downtown Coeur d'Alene, which is currently being revitalized.

As of the end of 1999, John Stone is again refocusing his development company by re-entering the Spokane-area development arena. The company is currently developing a new, high-tech park, in an attempt to assist in spurring economic growth and new technologies throughout the Spokane-area.

SPOKANE RAILWAY CREDIT UNION

Dedicated Aug. 6, 1929, on the eve of the Great Depression, the new Great Northern Railway Yards & Shops in Hillyard ushered in an industrious era for local railroad employees against a backdrop of harsh economic and social times in Spokane. In its prime, Great Northern employed 6,000 workers in Hillyard; the workshop crew was revered for its craftsmanship in building the giant steam locomotives known as Mallets.

In 1937, 73 enterprising railway workers pooled $493 in savings to form Great Northern Employees Credit Union. Financial cooperative organizations were gaining in popularity across the country, in part because of the economic hardships brought on by

SRCU's heritage is linked to Hillyard, once a booming railroad town. At one time, the credit union served members from a tiny office located above Hand's Drug Store at Market and Queen. Circa 1930s. Courtesy Cheney Cowles Museum.

the Depression. Credit unions often served as the only means for people to make ends meet—by merging their own resources to benefit one another. As a result, these organizations generated a spirit of camaraderie among members that extended to surrounding communities, with which they frequently formed close ties.

Great Northern Employees Credit Union served its first members (employees of Great Northern Railway and Spokane, Portland & Seattle Railway) from the Hillyard Depot. Over the years, the cooperative moved a number of times before settling into rented space at E. 3016 Queen Ave. in Hillyard in 1967.

Another cooperative, Railway Workers Credit Union, was founded in 1941 by 44 resourceful railroad employees, whose combined savings totaled $120 in credit union assets. The association served employees of Milwaukee Road, Northern Pacific Rail-

way, Railway Express Agency, Spokane International Railway, Union Pacific Railroad and other railways. Credit union business was conducted from a small room in the basement of a member's home on West Jackson Avenue.

Spokane benefited from the prosperity of a robust railway industry for many years. In the early 1970s, however, the industry began experiencing vast changes with profound consequences for the area and its railway-affiliated credit unions. Several major railroads consolidated, and in 1971 Amtrak took over much of the inner-city passenger train service throughout the United States. These and other changes reduced local railroad operations, resulting in a decline in the number of railway jobs in Spokane.

Great Northern Employees Credit Union (which had joined with Western Fruit Credit Union in 1968) and Railway Workers

Credit Union merged in 1970 under the name Spokane Railway Credit Union (SRCU). At that time, the organization had a combined membership of 3,486 and $2.4 million in assets.

In 1982 Burlington Northern Railroad (formerly Great Northern Railway, now Burlington Northern Santa Fe Railway) closed its Hillyard shops. That same year, SRCU's charter was amended to include in its field of membership employees of shippers of goods by rail or truck within the Inland Empire. This allowed SRCU to retain its strength and stability while facing a continuing decrease in the number of local railroad employees during the ensuing years.

Teamsters Local #690 was added to the cooperative's field of

membership in 1982; the following year, Teamsters Local #582 was included. Spokane Realty Credit Union liquidated its assets and merged with SRCU in 1983. In 1984 the Laborers Local 238 & 1151 Credit Union merged with SRCU. That same year, SRCU became the first financial institution in the Pacific Northwest to offer audio-response access to account information with the debut of its Satellite Teller.

Under the leadership of president and CEO Dennis A. Cutter, who joined SRCU in 1971, several Spokane communities have been added to the credit union's field of membership, allowing residents of the South Hill, Spokane Valley, Northeast Spokane, Indian Trail, and West Central areas to join the

Today, SRCU serves nearly 40,000 members from six full-service locations throughout the Inland Northwest.

credit union. An expanded membership base has enabled SRCU to prosper, while extending the benefits of credit union membership to thousands of Inland Northwest residents. By 1996 the cooperative exceeded $200 million in assets.

Spokane Railway Credit Union, founded on the "people-helping-people" credit union philosophy, continues to play a vital role in the Inland Empire. Today the credit union has more than $270 million in assets and serves nearly 40,000 members throughout the Inland Northwest. SRCU maintains five branch offices in the Spokane area and one branch office in Coeur d'Alene, Idaho.

TELECT, INC.

Telect's story is one of humble origins and rapid, exciting growth. In autumn 1982, Bill Williams Jr., his wife Judi, and their son Wayne opened Telect's doors in rented warehouse space in Spokane. When the U.S. government deregulated the telephone industry in the early 1980s, the Williams family and a financial partner generated the capital to launch Telect as a manufacturer of custom cable assemblies. Telect opened in 32,000 square-feet of leased space in the Spokane Industrial Park in the Spokane Valley, and the company's story began. Ten employees handled the first era of manufacturing at Telect, where the first month of operations grossed $10,000 in sales.

"In the first few months there were times when we had a few doubts," said Judi Williams, the company's co-founder and vice-chairman of the board. "But we had such great people here from the beginning, and that definitely helped the company succeed."

After starting exclusively as a cable company, Telect's product line quickly grew to include digital signal cross-connects, jackfields, and high and low-density bays for companies such as U.S. Sprint, Contel, RCA, and American Satellite. New products developed

Telect manufactures a comprehensive range of fiber optic products, as well as digital connectivity and power distribution systems for the communications industry.

Telect bases its worldwide operations in its Liberty Lake, Washington headquarters.

as customers communicated their needs—a process that still shapes Telect's product design today. Over the course of nearly 20 years of quality relationships with suppliers and customers, this handful of products has grown into a complete family of product lines for the communications industry, including fiber optic and digital access and cross-connect systems, power distribution and protection products, and cabling and accessory items.

By 1987, Telect supported more than 100 employees. Steady growth continued into the 1990s and fueled corporate expansion. Throughout the decade, Telect expanded its Liberty Lake, Washington headquarters, and in 1997, the company celebrated its 15th anniversary by creating an additional 120,000 square-feet of new manufacturing and administrative space at the existing headquarters location.

Today, Telect's worldwide family includes more than 1,000 employees and facilities in Southampton, England, Wroclaw, Poland, and Guadalajara, Mexico, in addition to Liberty Lake. Telect's products support large global Fortune 500 wireless and transmission product companies, and

primary markets include the Internet, wireless networks, telecommunications companies, CATV, government, education, and enterprise networks. All of this was created from the vision of three people.

"When we started Telect, we knew there was an opportunity for a company like the one we envisioned," says founder and chairman of the board Bill Williams, Jr. "We had no idea the opportunity would be so strong, however, and we're thankful every day for the hard work of all of our employees and the support of the greater Spokane community."

Principles in place since the beginning helped Telect reach its global status today. In an industry dominated by giants, Telect had to differentiate itself by the level of service it provided, in terms of quality products, customer service, and community involvement. Even as a multimillion-dollar company, serving its customers—and the communities in which it operates—is still and always at the forefront of all Telect processes, policies, and activities. These values will guide the company into its future as it continues to grow around the world.

TRANS-SYSTEM, INC.

Trans-System, Inc. currently consists of more than 800 trucks and three operating divisions: System Transport, a flatbed operation, TW Transport (TWT), a refrigerated and dry van operation, and James J. Williams, a bulk commodities hauling operation. Trans-System operates in the continental United States, Canada and Mexico and is supported by a national network of terminals and sales offices. James C. "Jim" Williams is Trans-System's chairman, chief executive officer and majority stockholder. Trans-System, Inc., has been served by hundreds of dedicated, hardworking, talented employees and owner operators, also by key executives including Dale Peterson, William Haley, Gary King, Jim Landwehr and Ted Rehwald.

Spokane's largest trucking company began a remarkably short time ago. In 1972, Jim Williams began operations as Interior Transport with one truck and one flatbed trailer. In 1973, he began TWT with two trucks and two trailers. The foundation for the double-digit annual growth that has been achieved has been Jim's entrepreneurial vision, excellent customers, invaluable business partners and the company's values. These five values are the principles that guide day-to-day operations and all business decisions, and they are: 1) the recognition that people are the company's most valuable asset; 2) the proper management and balance of innovation, creativity and risk taking; 3) the company's tradition of providing timely, dependable and knowledgeable customer service; 4) integrity and honesty in all business transactions; and 5) loyalty in all business relationships.

The company's growth has been additionally aided by the deregu-

"Joe" Williams with truck #1, 1938.

lation of the trucking industry in 1979 which created new opportunities for growth, also by some strategic acquisitions. In 1979, Interior Transport purchased the assets of System Transport, a national flatbed trucking company and it began operating under the System name and TWT acquired P. F. Huntley, Inc.

System and TWT trucks and trailers at new corporate headquarters grand opening in 1984.

In a sense, the origin of the company dates back to 1936. Jim's grandfather, James J. "Joe" Williams began a trucking company hauling petroleum products, servicing the Inland Northwest preceding World War II. The company grew, expanding into other commodities as demand for its high quality service increased. Joe Williams brought his son Dennis "Denny" Williams into the business and the business continued to prosper. The James J. Williams Trucking Company remained in the Williams Family until 1961 when it was sold after the premature death of Denny Williams. After several attempts the James J. Williams Trucking Company was successfully purchased by Trans-System, Inc. in 1996, bringing the company full circle and back into the Williams Family.

Now, the fourth generation of the Williams family in trucking is represented by Dennis Williams, Jim's son, and the traditions and values that have served Northwest's best trucking company so well will continue into the 21st century.

WHITWORTH COLLEGE

The story of Whitworth College begins in 1853, when George Whitworth, a minister in the Ohio Valley, headed west on the Oregon Trail to establish a college that would provide a "good English education and a thorough religious training." Once in the Pacific Northwest, Whitworth worked for over 30 years as a preacher, businessman and school superintendent, founded as many as 20 churches, and served as president of the nascent University of Washington.

Finally, in 1883, in the Washington Territory village of Sumner, Whitworth helped found Sumner Academy. Seven years later, in February 1890, the school was incorporated as Whitworth College. From the outset, Whitworth and other founding trustees aimed to build a college under the direction of the Presbyterian Church. They articulated a vision that committed to "guarding well the moral and religious life of the students, ever directing them in pursuit of that learning and culture of heart and mind that make the finished scholar." That belief in the education of the whole person—the education of both mind and heart—has provided the underlying vision for the college to this day.

While the rural environs of Sumner provided a pleasant environment for Whitworth's first students, financial difficulties encouraged trustees to look for a new location. In 1899, the college relocated to Tacoma and occupied the grandest mansion in the city. Whitworth students and faculty had a spectacular view of the Olympic Mountains, Commencement Bay and Mount Rainier. During this time, student traditions flourished, athletics teams competed against the universities of Oregon and Washington, a Whitworth student was named a Rhodes Scholar, and the college's commitment to academic excellence was established. Nevertheless, proper financial backing continued to prove problematic.

In 1914, trustees again decided to move the college—this time to Spokane. Encouraged by developer Jay P. Graves and the local presbytery, the college relocated to its current location in north Spokane. Having barely re-established itself in eastern Washington, Whitworth needed to close its doors during World War I because so many of its male students were called into service. The decade following the war proved especially difficult: enrollment was low and threats of merger and closure made the future uncer-

Whitworth students preparing to enlist in the First World War.

tain. Fire destroyed one of only two major buildings on campus in 1927. But, even in the midst of such uncertainty, Whitworth began to establish itself as a credible institution in Spokane. During the Great Depression of the 1930s, increasing numbers of Spokane students found their way to the college. At times, tuition could be paid only in produce and, by at least one student, in peanut butter. Nevertheless, President Ward Sullivan and Dean Francis Hardwick provided leadership that translated into greater stability and a more hopeful future.

In 1940 college trustees brought Dr. Frank Warren to Whitworth as its president. For the next 23 years, Warren oversaw the building of a substantial number of academic, dormitory, athletic, and administrative facilities. The modern campus began to take shape, and with the aid of the G-I Bill, enrollment grew rapidly. Warren centered the college around its mission and identity as a Christian college and established many of the distinctives that mark the institution to this day. Whitworth developed an outstanding athletics program in the 1950s, and professors Fenton Duvall in history and Clarence Simpson in English provided singular academic leadership and teaching expertise.

The tumultuous 1960s saw many changes at Whitworth, as at most colleges and universities across the country. Curriculum changes accompanied social changes as traditional rules and regulations gave way to the forces of change in American society. And yet the college, under President Mark Koehler, clung to its mission as a community of Christian scholars providing Whitworth's students a mind-and-heart education.

In 1970, Edward Lindaman assumed the presidency of Whitworth, and people in Spokane began to think of the college in new ways. Lindaman, known nationally for his futuristic thinking, encouraged the development of new and innovative student programs, fostered openness to new curricular ventures and broadened Whitworth's reach into the Spokane community.

Lindaman's successors, Robert Mounce and Arthur De Jong, added clarity of mission and increased support for international programs, including the Master of International Management Program, Whitworth's contribution to the larger initiative of the Spokane Intercollegiate Research and Technology Institute.

In 1990, Whitworth marked its centennial year with a capital campaign resulting in the construction of a greatly expanded and renovated library and student center. In 1993, William Robinson assumed the presidency and has led Whitworth to the strongest position in the college's history. Enrollment has reached 1,500 full-time undergraduate students and approximately 500 graduate students. Student retention and financial stability are at record levels. Whitworth's faculty is acknowledged regionally and nationally for its academic strength and Christian commitment, and Whitworth students have distinguished themselves in the arts, the sciences, and the helping professions.

Whitworth alumni can be found all over the world, and thousands of Whitworth graduates contribute to community life in Spokane. The college's current students are active in a number of local social services, including Habitat for Humanity and En Christo, a downtown hotel ministry to the poor. Having emerged as a significant educational and cultural force in the Spokane area and beyond, Whitworth looks forward to its opportunities to strengthen regional and national relationships in the 21st century, and to build upon its long and successful association with the City of Spokane.

Harriet Cheney Cowles Memorial Library, Whitworth campus.

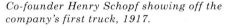

WILBERT PRECAST, INC.

Wilbert Precast, Inc. has been in business in Spokane for over 93 years. What began in 1906 as a local business primarily making burial vaults, has grown to a fourth-generation precast business that supplies a large variety of concrete products to eastern Washington, northern Idaho, and western Montana.

In 1904, Henry and John Schopf headed west from Indiana. They purchased a ranch near Republic, WA, and in 1906 founded Schopf & Co. Cement Contractors in Spokane. The original building was located at Broadway and Monroe. The brothers took turns running the ranch and the concrete business. John Schopf was an inventor, and he developed a new end-seal

Current President Dan Houk, age four, and brother Mark, six, watching contruction of new production facility on N. Cedar, 1962. Also pictured is their grandfather, William S. Houk and their father, William J. Houk.

concrete vault along with other specialty concrete products such as laundry trays and building systems. Henry Schopf was very involved in the business but was also able to serve as County

Co-founder Henry Schopf showing off the company's first truck, 1917.

Commissioner in Ferry County and during his term argued successfully for the building of the road over Sherman Pass.

In the early years, the vaults were delivered by horse and wagon. A vault delivery for L.L. Bruning Funeral Home in Colfax, only 60 miles away, required that the horse and wagon be loaded on a railroad flatcar for the ride to Colfax. The company purchased its first truck in 1917. Due to the nature of their business, John Schopf's daughter, Eva Mae, told how the family was able to get through the Depression by continuing to produce vaults and servicing the community. They were able to work when no one else was working.

In the early 1930s, a group of funeral homes owned the business, though it was still managed by John Schopf. The company was located at the sand pits just west of Division on Cora, and the name had changed to Spokane Concrete Vault Co. In the early 1940s, it moved to its present location at the 1300 block of North Cedar. The family regained ownership in the company when in the late 1940s the funeral homes put the business out for bid, and it was purchased by John Schopf's daughter and son-in-law, Eva and William S. Houk. Due to the advances in transportation over the years, vaults were now delivered to a wider geographic area. As with the Schopf brothers and still true today, vaults set at the cemeteries included a tent and chairs for the family members. William S. Houk continued to run the vault plant until it was sold in 1961 to his son, William J. Houk.

When William J. purchased the company it was a three-man operation, but was headed for big changes. William J. Houk began construction on a new concrete tilt-up building to expand their operation at North Cedar. He also purchased a franchise from Wilbert, Inc., the national leader in lined and sealed concrete burial vaults, and changed the company name to Spokane Wilbert Vault Co. This allowed the company the opportunity to offer families more options for funeral

Wilbert Precast, Inc.'s current facility on N. Cedar.

Erecting precast wall panels on 10,000 square-foot building in order to relocate Wilbert's Lewiston operation, 1999.

services. Wilbert vaults are hand-painted in a two-color process to match the family's choice of casket, and liner options including stainless steel, copper, or bronze are available. The delivery range grew to include all of western Montana. An additional building was added in 1970, and in 1977 the company began to diversify into septic tanks, drywells, catch basins, and related products.

William J. Houk had graduated from WSU with a degree in architecture in 1952, but had put that career on hold when he purchased the

business from his parents. In 1983, he stepped down from the daily operations and his son Dan T. Houk became general manager. In the 20+ years that William J. Houk was at the helm, the sales figures doubled nearly every five years. He was able to return to architecture and designed several mausoleums for area cemeteries, with Spokane Wilbert Vault Co. providing the concrete components for these projects. He retired from the company in 1992.

Spokane Wilbert Vault Co. added additional plants in Yakima and Lewiston in 1985, adding a new product line of precast steps and wrought iron railings. The company also became general contractors for constructing the mausoleums and for building large water reservoirs and septic tank systems. The company expanded again in 1997 when it added manholes to its list of products, and in 1999, a new plant was added in Wenatchee.

In January 1999 the name changed to Wilbert Precast, Inc. to reflect the changes of the company over the last 30+ years. Today, Wilbert Precast, Inc. sits on 8.5 acres at the North Cedar site, employs approximately 50 people and has a fleet of about 25 trucks traveling the northwest highways. The longevity of the company, according to President Dan T. Houk, is attributed to the company's custom of doing everything in its power to meet the needs of its customers. Wilbert Precast, Inc. and its fine employees will continue that tradition for many years to come.

WITHERSPOON, KELLEY, DAVENPORT & TOOLE, P.S.

George M. Forster, one of the founders of Witherspoon, Kelley, Davenport & Toole, P.S., arrived in Spokane in 1883. He traveled from the Mississippi Valley to the Pacific Northwest with his brother-in-law W.W. Witherspoon. Since 1883 was the year the Transcontinental Railroad linked to the Northern Pacific railroad, it is likely that it was the mode of travel they chose.

Spokane was a frontier town settled by people attracted to this fertile area rich in natural resources. Water was abundant. Spokane is located near the junction of the Spokane and Columbia Rivers. Rich Silver and lead deposits were located in Northern Idaho and British Columbia. Spokane Falls and close proximity to the mines created two natural advantages in the settlement of Spokane.

Spokane was founded in 1873, just 10 years prior to George M. Forster's arrival. It presented a golden opportunity for a young attorney. In 1884 Forster formed a partnership with Colonel W.W.D. Turner and founded the law practice of Turner and Forster. They were pioneers in establishing a law firm in this frontier town.

Forster was also one of the founding owners of the well known Le Roi Mining and Smelting Company in Rossland. He was instrumental in shaping the Spokane business community.

Forster was recognized for his integrity. Judge George Turner was appointed associate justice of the Supreme Court of the Washington Territory in 1884 and assigned to the fourth district, which covered much of eastern Washington. He subsequently moved to Spokane. In 1887 Judge Turner resigned his judicial position to enter private

law practice. He joined his brother W.W.D. Turner and George Forster, in the law firm Turner and Forster. The firm then became known as Turner, Forster and Turner. He remained with the law firm until 1890.

Judge Turner played a prominent role in shaping the destiny of the State of Washington. The Washington territory began to grow rapidly with the completion of the Northern Pacific Railroad in 1883. Statehood came soon after, in 1889.

As chairman of the judiciary committee at the constitutional convention Judge Turner played a key role in forming the Washington State constitution. Judge Turner was later elected U. S. Senator from Washington. He considered public service a privilege and served his constituency well, also becoming prominent in national affairs.

Shortly after Judge Turner left the law firm in 1890, his brother Colonel W.W.D. Turner retired. During the period from 1891-92 Colonel Turner retired and a new partnership was formed between George M. Forster and W.J.C. Wakefield.

W.J.G. Wakefield completed his study of law in the office of Archer and Bowden in San Jose, California. In early 1889 he was

Judge George Turner. Courtesy, Northwest Room, Spokane Public Library

admitted to the bar in San Francisco, California. He then moved on to the Pacific Northwest and settled in Spokane. In November 1889 Wakefield formed a partnership with Judge L.B. Nash, with whom he practiced law until the spring of 1892. He then succeeded Colonel W.W.D. Turner and the law firm Turner and Forster became Forster and Wakefield.

When an individual studies the law while working in a law firm in the company of an attorney or group of attorneys, it is called reading the law. Archibald W. Witherspoon, related by marriage to George Forster, began his law reading under the direction of Forster and Wakefield in 1895. He was admitted to the bar in January 1899.

Forster, the last original founder of the Spokane law firm, died in 1905. The law firm then became Wakefield and Witherspoon. Witherspoon was an attorney and a businessman. He was chairman of the board of the Old National Bank.

Wakefield died in 1931 and sometime after that the firm became known as Witherspoon, Witherspoon and Kelley. A.W. Witherspoon's son William W. joined the law firm in the late 1920s.

Today the law firm of Witherspoon, Kelley, Davenport & Toole,

W. J. G. Wakefield. Courtesy, Northwest Room, Spokane Public Library

P.S. is a professional service corporation. It is the second oldest law firm in the state and the oldest law firm in the city of Spokane. At this writing there are 38 attorneys in the firm, five of whom have been with the firm 30 years each or more. Witherspoon, Kelley, Davenport & Toole, P.S. continues to maintain the integrity of its founders and takes pride in the integrity it has maintained over the years. It continues to provide quality legal service and support to the Spokane-area and continues to be an integral part of its growth. An office was established in Coeur d'Alene in 1987 in order to better serve the Inland Empire.

The firm is presently located in the U.S. Bank Building, formerly the Old National Bank Building. Until 1946 the offices were located in the Peyton Building near the railroad tracks, where the members of the firm suffered the inconvenience

George Forster. Courtesy, Northwest Room, Spokane Public Library

of coal dust settling on their books and papers.

Witherspoon, Kelley, Davenport & Toole, P.S., will carry its 100-year heritage of quality, expert legal services at cost-effective rates into the 21st century and beyond.

The attorneys and counselors of Witherspoon, Kelley, Davenport and Toole, P.S. are experienced in banking, bankruptcy, business litigation, condemnation, construction, corporate, employee benefit plans, employment and labor, environmental, health care, insurance defense (including medical malpractice and product liability), land-use planning, media, mergers & acquisitions, probate, real estate, securities, taxation (individual, corporate, estate & gift), trial practice, and zoning law.

WASHINGTON TRUST BANK

Founded in Spokane in 1902, the Washington Trust Company opened at 115 Mill Street, soon to be renamed "Wall" Street. The founders had a vision to serve the financial needs of local people and businesses in the prosperous Spokane community, and to do so with the best customer service possible. The Stanton family has been involved with the Bank since E. H. Stanton bought controlling interest in 1912. Today, president and chairman Peter Stanton is the fourth generation of the family to lead the bank.

As Washington Trust grew through the roaring '20s, trust in this local business grew as well. Washington Trust was known for integrity and principle. The Bank earned an enviable reputation during the Depression, when it met every request for withdrawal of funds, and remained open. Long-time customers still talk about it today.

The success of Washington Trust in weathering the Depression and maintaining the public's

Washington Trust Bank lobby in its prior headquarters, circa 1930s.

faith through some of our nation's darkest financial times spurred more growth. In 1932 Washington Trust moved to a new, larger headquarters at 715 West Sprague, and by 1941 assets exceeded $10 million. Frederick Stanton was elected president that year, succeeding his father, and at age 54, became the youngest bank president ever in Spokane.

After World War II, Washington Trust experienced even greater, sustained success and in 1950 became the first bank in Spokane to open a drive-in branch. The innovative, customer-service oriented bank continues to offer new banking products and features. By the early 1960s Wash-

ington Trust had expanded its branch bank system to four locations, and Philip Stanton, at age 31, succeeded his father as bank president—another new record for youth in this position.

Under Phil Stanton's leadership, Washington Trust grew to 16 branches with assets of $440 million, and in 1974 opened a new headquarters, the Washington Trust Financial Center, at 717 West Sprague. In 1984, the Bank's strong commitment and history of support for the communities it serves was recognized by a prestigious award from the State of Washington. In 1990, Peter Stanton, age 34, became president, and, while not breaking his father's record, was the *second* youngest bank president in Spokane history.

The '90s saw great growth for Washington Trust Bank, in terms of assets, branches, services, innovations and geographic scope. The Bank expanded to central Washington and northern Idaho, for a total of 28 branches in 1999. Today, Washington Trust is the largest full-service commercial bank headquartered in the state of Washington. Still true to its original mission, Washington Trust provides high-quality financial products and services to individuals and businesses through a network of convenient branch locations as well as through telephone banking and on-line internet banking services. The Bank has also earned a reputation for having superior commercial, private banking and trust departments.

As Washington Trust Bank enters the new millennium, it continues its mission of extraordinary customer service and sustained financial leadership in the communities it serves.

Current lobby of Washington Trust Bank's headquarters at 717 W. Sprague Avenue.

ZAK DESIGNS, INC.

Zak Designs, the world's leading distributor of licensed children's and adult dinnerware has been an established business for over 23 years.

In 1976, Irv Zakheim established Patchwork Designs. A forerunner to Zak Designs, Patchwork Designs created and imported handmade pillows, baby quilts and Christmas items.

By 1980, with his overseas contacts well established, Zakheim switched his company's focus to kitchenware, and changed the name to Zak Designs, Inc. The company enjoyed substantial growth over the next few years, adding a full-range of kitchen items. In 1984, Zakheim created the first Zak Zany Zoo Animal Oven Mitt. The mitts ultimately gave Zakheim an entry into the licensed children's dinnerware and drinkware market.

The company successfully manufactured and distributed children's dinnerware featuring various licenses for the next few years. In 1988, Zak Designs picked up its first license from *Disney Consumer Products, Chip n'Dale Rescue Rangers*. Then came other popular licenses such as *The Little Mermaid*, followed by *101 Dalmatians, Barbie, Batman, Looney*

Irv Zakheim, founder, president and CEO of Zak Designs, Inc.

Tunes, Winnie the Pooh and *Mickey Mouse* among others. Currently, Zak Designs distributes children's, infant, and adult dinnerware featuring over 40 different licenses.

In 1992, Zak Designs relocated their corporate headquarters and distribution center to Spokane, from Los Angeles. After one year Zak Designs grew from five to 48 employees and total sales grew 26 percent. "Since moving to the Spokane area, we've done nothing but grow and expand," commented Irv Zakheim, President/CEO of Zak Designs. In 1995, Zak De-

signs was listed as one of *Inc.* Magazine's Top 500 Fastest Growing Private Companies in the United States. Today, Zak Designs employs over 180 people and continues to experience double digit annual sales growth. To accommodate this growth, Zak Designs has undergone seven expansions to its warehouse and office facilities since its relocation to the Spokane area.

Today, Zak Designs products can be found at most major retailers throughout the United States, in addition to many retailers in Canada, Europe, Japan, Italy and Mexico. Currently, in the United States alone, the list includes more than 5,000 retail stores of all categories.

Zak Designs expanded their market presence in April 1997 with the acquisition of Selandia Designs, a housewares leader in the department store, specialty and gift market. The company acquired the assets of stainless steel housewares producer Möller Designs USA, Inc. in 1998, and Treasure Craft, a Southern California-based ceramic cookie jar and accessories producer, in 1999.

Along with corporate success, Zak Designs remains highly involved within the Spokane community. Mr. Zakheim is on the board of directors for the Spokane Chamber of Commerce, Boy Scouts of America, YMCA, and The United Way. He is the driving force behind Zak Designs' participation in numerous community efforts including Toys for Tots, The Commute Trip Reduction Campaign, The Spokane Food Bank, The Wishing Star Foundation, and The United Way.

Since 1976, Zak Designs has grown from a small, unknown distributor into one of Washington's top 150 privately held companies.

Corporate headquarters for Zak Designs, Inc. in Spokane, WA.

SOURCES FOR FURTHER STUDY

There is room to mention only a fraction of the sources which went into the making of this book, so I'll emphasize those I found most helpful and/or those which seem to me would be valuable further reading.

All historians of Spokane start with N.W. Durham's three-volume *History of the City of Spokane and Spokane County, Washington, From Its Earliest Settlement to the Present Time* (S.J. Clark Publishing Co., 1912). Though lacking in objectivity, the work is a valuable source of raw material. Durham was an early editor of the *Spokesman-Review* and knew many of the people and events he writes about. Another valuable source of information is a chronicle called *Story of Spokane,* compiled by Orville Pratt, a one-time superintendent of Spokane schools. Pratt's notes about developments in Spokane up to the year 1948 are unpublished, but bound typescripts are available through the Spokane Public Libraries. A well-written (though somewhat out-of-date) regional history is George W. Fuller's *History of the Pacific Northwest, With Special Emphasis on the Inland Empire* (Alfred A. Knoff, 1948). The pattern of eastern Washington's development is told in a fascinating book by D.W. Meinig called *The Great Columbia Plain: A Historical Geography 1805-1910* (University of Washington, 1968).

Two Spokane historians, Jay J. Kalez and Roland Bond, have written several anecdotal histories of Spokane which are well worth reading. I used Kalez' *Saga of a Western Town, 1882-1972* (Lawton Publishing Co., 1972) and Bond's *Early Birds In The Northwest* (Enterprises Press, 1971). Another local historian who has contributed mightily to Spokane's small shelf of history is Wilfred Schoenberg, S.J. I consulted especially his *Gonzaga University* (published by Gonzaga University, 1963).

No one writes so authoritatively about the all-important mining history of the area as John Fahey. I used his *Inland Empire: D.C. Corbin and Spokane* (University of Washington Press, 1965) and *The Ballyhoo Bonanza: Charles Sweeney and the Idaho Mines* (University of Washington Press, 1971).

Barbara F. Cochran's *Exploring Spokane's Past* (Ye Galleon Press, 1979) is an excellent and accurate walking tour guide to Spokane's historic monuments. An interesting recent addition to Spokane history is Robert B. Hyslop's *Spokane Building Blocks* (available in manuscript at the Cheney Cowles Museum and elsewhere, 1983). Hyslop, an architect, traces the changes of buildings of every downtown address over the period of a century.

The story of the great flood which shaped so much of eastern Washington's landscape is clearly and succinctly told by Harlan J. Bretz in *Washington's Channeled Scablands* (Washington State Government publication, 1959). The discovery and significance of the Marmes archaeological dig is summarized in *The Oldest Man In America* (Harcourt, Brace, Jovanovich, 1970) by Ruth Kirk. Customs of this region's Indians are briefly described in *Children of the Sun: A History of the Spokane Indians* by David C. Wynecoop (published by the author, 1969) and *Manners and Customs of the Coeur d' Alene Indians* by Jerome Peltier (also published by the author, 1975). Two books which purportedly describe the Indian, but reflect much about whites, are *Nine Years with The Spokane Indians: The Diary of Elkanah Walker, 1838-1848,* compiled by Clifford M. Drury (Arthur H. Clark Co., 1976) and *Sketches of Indian Life In The Pacific Northwest* by Alexander Diomedi, S.J., (Ye Galleon Press, 1978), edited by Edmund J. Kowrach, S.J.

Three books are indispensable to understanding the area's Indian wars: the relevant chapters of *The Life of Isaac Ingalls Stevens,* written by his son, Hazard Stevens, who was with his father in these years and thus was an eyewitness (Houghton, Mifflin, 1901); *Ka-Mi-Akin* by A.J. Splawn (Caxton Printers, 1958), a flattering biography of a warrior to balance his treatment by most white historians; and B.J. Manring's *The Conquest of the Coeur d' Alenes, Spokanes and Palouses* (John W. Graham and Co., 1912), a balanced description of Colonel George Wright's campaign which cites original sources at length. Anyone seriously interested in local Indian history may want to consult the interviews and profiles in the collected papers of William F. Lewis, an attorney who early in this century did the community a great service by interviewing many Indians and pioneers.

Much of the early history of the city was fitted together bit by bit from diaries, letters and newspaper reminiscences to be found under pioneer names in the Cheney Cowles Museum. These are the sources of much of the information on Glover, Keats, Nosler and Campbell, to name a few. Though not published, these are accessible to anyone and make delightful reading. Aspects of Spokane's turn-of-the-century economics and social life are treated in *The Economic History of Spokane, Wa., 1881-1910,* a 1962 Gonzaga University doctoral thesis by William H. Kensel, and the *Age of Elegance* by Margaret Bean (Eastern Washington Historical Society, 1968).

One runs into a special problem in writing about the Cowles family. There are no family papers in the Cheney Cowles Museum and almost no articles have been written about them. The only book about the family, Ralph E. Dyar's *News For An Empire* (Caxton Press, 1952), was commissioned by the family. It is full of specific information, but of course is uncritical. I found useful a thesis at Washington State University, *The Spokesman-Review, 1883-1900, A Mirror To The History of Spokane* (1967) by Robert A. Henderson.

Two books on fascinating sideshows of the 1920s are *Rum Road To Spokane* (University of Montana, 1972) by Edmund Fahey, who tells his own story as a Prohibition-era supplier of liquor, and *Lionhead Lodge* by Lloyd Peters (Ye Galleon Press, 1976), a firsthand account about Spokane's brief flirtation with the movie business. Most of the handful of biographies of Bing Crosby briefly describe his Spokane boyhood,

but the only book I found useful on the topic was his autobiography, *Call Me Lucky* (Simon and Schuster, 1953). The information about Crosby came mostly from interviews of those who knew him here, which I have treated at more length elsewhere (*Spokane Magazine,* December, 1977).

Even the contemporary newspapers shed little light on the conditions in Spokane during the Depression. A bibliography at Washington State University (Balzarini, S.E., "A Select List of Business and Other Records of the Depression Era in the WSU Libraries") provided some help, especially a 1937 summary of the city's participation in federal recovery programs called "City Progress Contest."

Descriptions of the Spokane home front during World War II were gleaned from contemporary newspaper accounts. Fairchild Air Force Base's official history, *1942-1982: Sentinel of the Pacific Northwest* by La Rine McGimpsey and Bill Harris was helpful with the background of that important part of the community. Stories of Spokane units and men overseas came from newspaper reports, interviews, and unit records. Notable in the last category is the four volumes of records on the 161st Infantry, Washington National Guard, compiled by William Bateman, historian of the unit.

The important question of the fifties and sixties, the Spokane economy, is well documented, though in sources not easily available. A series of reports called "Economic and Business Studies—State College of Washington," lo-

cated in the Washington State University library, looks at many aspects of the Spokane economy in the decade following the war. Gonzaga University business students have contributed a series of invaluable theses concerning Spokane's economy and public attitudes toward it through the 1960s. Spokane Unlimited commissioned studies by the economic planning firms of Larry Smith, Inc. and EBASCO Services. The studies are available in the Spokane Main Branch library. The problem of sprawling suburbs is documented in any number of city and county reports, namely "Subdivision Activity, 1950-1957" (Spokane County Government, 1959). The change of form of government in 1960 is interestingly sketched in a handy volume of newspaper clippings called *The League of Women Voters Clipping and Materials Book, 1960,* which is available at Eastern Washington University. The politics of the mid-1960s are examined in a collection of papers called *Background Papers on Spokane* produced by the Eastern Washington University Community Services Institute (1967).

The seminal document of Expo '74, laying out the ground plan, is "Plan and Feasibility of Proposed Spokane Ecology Exposition" (Economics Research Associates, 1970). But there is no good comprehensive history of the Expo effort. The material in this book came almost entirely from newspaper clippings and interviews with Expo planners.

ACKNOWLEDGMENTS

I received a remarkable amount of help in writing this book. I want to thank Dr. Dale Stradling of Eastern Washington University for tutoring sessions on Spokane's geological history; Ruth Maston of EWU for her advice on Indian ethnology; and John Flett of the Spokane Indian Tribe, who could describe for me, from personal experience, Indian life both ancient and modern. Betty O'Laughlin went to extraordinary lengths of help me gather representative stories of Spokane's World War II veterans. In updating the section on James Gover, I had the help of a tireless researcher, Jean Oton. Nancy Gale Compau of the Spokane Public Library made her usual generous contributions to yet one more Spokane history project.

The editor of the original book, Pam Schroeder, was an amiable and helpful colleague. The editor of this revised edition, Carolyn Martin, contributed immeasurably with her enthusiasm, patience, and hard work. It was a pleasure to work with her.

My mother, Francis Stimson, called upon friendships that included a good portion of the Spokane population to find sources, facts, and photographs, which were invaluable to the book.

My wife Kristine was a full partner in this project. She conducted interviews, tracked down photographs, and, at the other end of the project, read and critiqued every page of the manuscript.

The original version of this book was dedicated to William Stimson, Jr., "and all the other juniors in Spokane." Since then we have been joined by Brie Stimson, who seems to have been born with an abiding interest in Western pioneers. My hope for all the juniors of Spokane is that they take the time to appreciate what those who went before them accomplished, and then that they go on to do even better.

William L. Stimson
Spokane, Washington

Kirtland Cutter bought a small cottage on the corner of Howard Street and Seventh Avenue and transformed it into his "Chalet Hohenstein," the first Swiss-style chalet in the U.S. (EWSHS)

INDEX